Contexts in Literature

Contemporary Fiction: The Novel since 1990

Pamela Bickley

Series editor: Adrian Barlow

CAMBRIDGE
UNIVERSITY PRESS

CAMBRIDGE UNIVERSITY PRESS

Cambridge, New York, Melbourne, Madrid, Cape Town, Singapore, São Paulo, Delhi

Cambridge University Press
The Edinburgh Building, Cambridge CB2 8RU, UK

www.cambridge.org
Information on this title: www.cambridge.org/9780521712491

First published 2008

Printed in the United Kingdom at the University Press, Cambridge

A catalogue record for this publication is available from the British Library

ISBN 978-0-521-71249-1 paperback

Editorial management: Gill Stacey

Cover illustration: © OJO Images Ltd / Alamy

Contents

Introduction

Post-1990 fiction is an exciting and rewarding area of study. Following a period when the decline of the novel was widely discussed, fiction has emerged as a vibrant and inventive genre, exploring the diversity of the contemporary world and frequently experimenting with form and language. This is not to say that current works of prose fiction are always optimistic and uplifting, there are few utopian worlds to discover. Rather, it might seem that the visions of urban decay, individual isolation and fractured relationships depict a bleak picture at the turn of the millennium. But readers will also find strange and compelling tales, new and original voices, trenchant wit and humour. Contemporary writing is a controversial area and readers will inevitably become involved in discussions over literary language and subject matter. It is precisely because modern writing engages with the new that it can be seen as challenging and, at times, disturbing. The post-1990 novel is expressive of a wide range of imaginative perspectives, both realist and fantastical. Post-colonial writing explores experiences of exile and displacement where the central question 'Who am I?' is probed and questioned. Some commentators have seen the numbers of novels taking as subject the two world wars of the 20th century as an obsession of contemporary writers. We live in troubled times and apocalyptic fears haunt certain texts as they grapple with the dark question of what happens beyond the end of civilised society.

This study intends to introduce readers to major and recurrent preoccupations of the post-1990 novel, to identify some of the chief characteristics of the genre, and to offer ways in which contemporary writing can be analysed and discussed.

Part 1: Reading contemporary fiction addresses the question of the genre itself, looking at the circumstances in which novels are written and received. Why does the novel continue to flourish in a world of increasingly sophisticated media? Can it still be seen as a form which can achieve novel, in the sense of 'new', effects? Fiction is constantly under discussion in today's society: from the media coverage of the prize world to local book groups, novels are regarded as significant. Clearly, novels arise out of their cultural moment; they might also be seen as shaping and crystallising that moment. Contemporary novelists such as Ian McEwan, Martin Amis, Graham Swift locate their fictions firmly within the recognisable modern world, as though insisting upon the 'real' in their work. James Kelman and Irvine Welsh have united a pursuit of narrative truth with the desire to challenge and unsettle readers, raising the question of whether the novel has reached the ultimate limits of expression and subject matter. New voices within contemporary writing introduce dual, or multiple, perspectives upon the modern world, and fiction. Hanif Kureishi, Zadie Smith, Kazuo Ishiguro, Michael Ondaatje belong to the post-1990 'novel in English', but their individual influences derive from many different sources. Cultural hybridity has proved to be part of the novel's continuing evolution and inventiveness. As well as examining some areas of the novel's production and reception, together with the relationship between contemporary writing and society, Part 1 also identifies thematic considerations which recur insistently in the writing of the late 20th century. Millennial anxiety inevitably informs writing which follows the 9/11 attacks on New York, yet the proliferation of novels revisiting the two great conflicts of the 20th century suggests that the past also remains troubling and unresolved.

Part 2: Approaches to the texts offers ways of analysing the form of the novel, considering narratives and narrators, plot and structure, types of 'characterisation'. Investigation of conventional areas of narration reveals the extent to which contemporary fiction experiments with inherited forms, or seeks to invent new strategies. Intertextuality is an experimental device which is characteristic of post-1990 writing. This section also examines different types of narrative realism – from the novelist's desire to insist upon factual accuracy (in McEwan's or Pat Barker's writing) to the bizarre world of Yann Martel's *Life of Pi*. Post-colonial writing is complex and varied, and different perspectives are explored here: the brutal, post-apartheid world of J.M. Coetzee's *Disgrace* as well as contemporary multicultural London in the writing of Monica Ali and Zadie Smith. The Irish rejection of British rule which informs the subtle and probing writing of William Trevor and Colm Tóibín is also relevant to this debate. Structural and thematic questions are illustrated with reference to a range of post-1990 writing, drawing on texts specified by UK examining boards as well as relevant comparative texts. Tasks and assignments suggest further reading as well as areas for discussion.

Part 4: Critical approaches examines the nature of textual interpretation: What expectations do readers bring to a given text? Is it appropriate to regard literature as enshrining timeless feelings and values? Discussion of Jane Smiley's *A Thousand Acres* demonstrates ways in which a single text may be open to multiple interpretations and differing critical views.

Most of the texts cited in this book belong to the category of 'contemporary British fiction'. Limitations of space preclude discussion of other writing in English, although some American novels have been included. Irish writing, for reasons belonging to history, is also included, although many Irish writers would claim a distinctly un-English tradition.

One of the advantages of studying the new and modern is that, although there may be relevant resources to consult, it is unlikely that students will find an overwhelming body of critical material. The novels are written for contemporary readers and the response of those readers is paramount.

How this book is organised

Part 1: Reading contemporary fiction
This section addresses key questions which dominate discussions of the genre, and identifies characteristic preoccupations of the novel in this period.

Part 2: Approaching the texts
This section introduces different ways in which fictional texts can be analysed, through discussion of a range of literary works.

Part 3: Texts and extracts
Part 3 offers a selection of extracts, chosen to illustrate different types of writing in the period. The extracts can be used as a basis for textual analysis and discussion.

Part 4: Critical approaches to contemporary fiction
In this section, different critical perspectives are introduced with some discussion of how these can be applied to specific texts.

Part 5: How to write about contemporary fiction
Part 5 aims to offer advice about structuring written work on fictional texts, using a range of suggested assignments.

Part 6: Resources
This section includes suggested further reading on the novel, a brief glossary of relevant critical terms and a chronology listing texts cited in the book with brief reference to contextual information.

1 Reading contemporary fiction

- Can the novel still be 'novel'?

- Book or Internet?

- Is there a modern literary canon?

- Is the novel in Britain obsessed with the historical past?

- How does the novel reflect its society?

Is the novel 'novel'?

The novel is the youngest literary **genre**: poetry and drama both have ancient roots in pre-Christian societies, evolving throughout the history of Western Europe. In England, the novel is usually dated from the beginning of the 18th century with the writing of Daniel Defoe (1660–1731), including *Robinson Crusoe* (1719) and *Moll Flanders* (1722). Many literary historians would regard the Victorian age as belonging pre-eminently to the novel, the Brontës, Dickens and George Eliot being undoubtedly the literary giants of their age. Today, equally, the novel as a form clearly dominates the publishing scene and, despite rival media attractions, remains popular. Has the novel, then, re-invented itself in order to survive, or does it retain traditional methods and styles?

Some of Britain's principal contemporary writers make great claims for the power of the novel. In the following comment, Salman Rushdie refers to the novel's capacity to be experimental in form, as well as challenging in its vision:

> I do not believe that novels are trivial matters. The ones I care most about are those which attempt radical reformulations of language, form and ideas, those that attempt to do what the word *novel* seems to insist upon: to see the world anew.

To Rushdie, the novel is an imaginative space offering unlimited freedom. Contemporary novels can range from realistic accounts of the First World War, based on authentic historical sources, to fantastical evocations of non-existent worlds in unknown galaxies. Stylistically, novels can be written in beautifully crafted language, with eloquent sentences that seem close to the effects of poetry. Or the language can be direct, brutal to a point that some readers will find offensive. In terms of form, novelists can choose to structure their material sequentially, with events unfolding in a logical order. Equally, form can be fragmented and apparently incoherent to suit particular **narrative** purposes.

For many writers, the crucial experience of the novel is that of the individual reader responding to the fictional world created. To the novelist Graham Swift

> [The] whole point of fiction … is to get away from yourself into experiences of other people, into different worlds, into different lives … It's all about imagining what it's like to be somebody else. And that is, after all, one of the most important tasks of life. One of the things the novel can do, is to stimulate that process.

Swift is arguing here that the novel has the ability to enlarge private, imaginative experience; other writers would argue that the novel plays its part within society, by shaping or challenging readers' perceptions. It is a long time since D.H. Lawrence (1885–1930) proposed the novel as 'the book of life', urging his readers to 'learn from the novel … see wherein you are [alive]', but it remains true that the moral concerns within certain novels are regarded as important and receive serious discussion. So the novel is still seen as offering unique fictional adventure or provocative ethical debate. The possibilities of the genre are not yet exhausted. The Czech novelist Milan Kundera has argued in his recent work *The Art of the Novel* that the novel has barely begun to explore its unlimited opportunities for narrative experimentation, particularly with concepts of thought, time, dream and mental play. But the vitality of the contemporary novel should not be taken for granted.

▶ Look at the reviews of Ishiguro's *Never Let Me Go* (pages 112–114) and discuss ways in which a novel might spark, or make a contribution to, ethical debate.

The death of the novel?

In 1980 the literary journal *Granta* debated the death of the novel in English, and the artistic and intellectual timidity of English writers. Citing major 20th-century critics, *Granta*'s editor Bill Buford accused the English novel of having a 'dreadful droning sameness', and being an essentially middle-class (whining) monologue, no more than 'a longish piece of writing with something wrong with it'. Worse, he argued, publishing was driven by consumer choice:

> Of course, it is a commonplace that what is published in the end is decided by the Great British Public. A mythic beast of extraordinary proportions – with puppy white arms, sustained by McVities chocolate biscuits and books about the Queen Mother.

In short, Buford's perception was that 'the novel is no longer novel' – a phrase coined by the critic Bernard Bergonzi in his survey of the genre, *The Situation of the Novel* (1970). As a form, the novel 'no longer possesses the essential "novelty" that traditionally characterised it'. During the post-war period, a number of writers tolled the funeral bell for fictional writing. The American critic Leslie Fieldler identified and lamented, in *Waiting for the End* (1965), a cultural moment which he termed 'the nausea of the end'. In *Granta*, Buford's strongest condemnation was for lack of experimentation with the form of the novel: too many fictions of the second half of the 20th century, he argued, seemed to be written in straightforward linear form. Texts failed to challenge readers, unwilling to disturb the artifice of 'character' and illusion of narrative certainty.

Towards the end of the 20th century, this critical consensus, that the novel has had its day, began to shift. The academic and critic Chris Bigsby, offering an analysis of the 'uneasy middle-ground' of British fiction, began to question the assumption that the novel is a 'cosily provincial, deeply conservative, anti-experimental enterprise, resistant to innovation, rooted in mimesis, dedicated to the preservation of a [19th century] tradition of realism'. He conceded the centrality of narrative and survival of character, but also identified an awareness of what he identified as 'textual insecurities':

> ... the suspect nature of language, the manipulative power of art, the fragility of character, the dubious nature of historicism, the relativity of value and perception, and the collapse of the absolute.
>
> *(Granta*, 1980)

How, then, has the contemporary novel survived a demoralising decline into torpor and stagnation?

Surveying these pessimistic judgements from the perspective of the 21st century is an intriguing business. There would seem to be few voices now to endorse such funereal pronouncements. In *How to Read a Novel* (2006), John Sutherland's opening chapter is entitled 'So many novels, so little time'. He observes that Samuel Johnson, in the 18th century – the period in which the novel as we understand it evolved – might conceivably expect to read all the major publications of his day. Now, more novels are published every week than Johnson would have encountered in a decade. According to the consumer research agency, BML, women bought 188 million fictional works in the UK in 2006 (8% more than in 2005), while men purchased 128 million. Setting aside any gender question implied here, or what kinds of fiction are included in these numbers, these figures show the immense popularity of the genre.

It would seem that, just as the death-throes of the novel are being announced, the genre is entering a vibrant period of revitalisation. Why this should have occurred towards the end of the 20th century is perhaps a simple question, but one which eludes simple answers. Any study of the modern novel must acknowledge at an early stage that it is an endlessly controversial area, and there is little settled consensus of opinion. Dominic Head in his conclusion to the *Cambridge History of Modern British Fiction* (2002) asserts that:

[The] novel of post-war history and society in Britain has been phenomenally rich and inventive, a genre in a state of creative expansion, and as far removed from terminal decline as it is possible to imagine.

Glittering prizes

So, although the 'death of the novel' has been a reiterated theme of the second half of the 20th century, the vast commercial success of the novel would seem to be unarguable. There is widespread familiarity with the Man Booker Prize, the Costa Book Awards (previously the Whitbread), and the Orange and James Tait Black Fiction Prizes, to name a few of the major English awards, and with the American Pulitzer and National Book Award. The Pulitzer and the Nobel Prize are possibly the high points of international success. The publication of a new novel is now an event of the media and the market place; it is no longer solely the business of academe or a select band of critics. David Lodge, in *The Practice of Writing* (1996), looks across twenty years of creative writing courses and observes how recent is the concept of the literary bestseller – he identifies this as a commercial event of the 1980s. In its earliest years (the late 1960s) the Booker Prize had no real impact on sales, but it subsequently developed the power to launch a bestseller. Now, it might be questioned whether literary texts have been selected for contemporary readers by the marketing body who advise major bookshops which titles to display at the entrance to their shops. Some will argue that this means an inevitable 'dumbing down' of material, and that a small clique of authors reappear on these annual shortlists and their current writing dominates publishing lists. A worst-case argument might go so far as to propose that subject matter and style are dictated by the prize mentality (or by TV chat-show presenters), with a certain degree of experimentation, but not too much. The author Julian Barnes has famously rejected the Booker Prize as 'Posh bingo'. More positively, it could be proposed that there is currently a renaissance of interest in fiction: book groups thrive and, undoubtedly, novels do sell. Books, then, occupy a public dimension: they are reviewed, discussed on TV and are available from supermarkets – they are not an elitist product reserved for a minority. Robert McCrum, the literary editor of the *Observer*, argued recently that the prize world does have its importance in recognising important contemporary writing:

Publishing, which is just another mirror to our society, cannot escape the zeitgeist. Prizes and their attendant hullabaloo satisfy contemporary narcissism and global consumerism in any number of ways. I would argue that they also play an indispensable role in identifying new writing of consequence.

(*The Observer*, 6 May 2007)

Hermione Lee, as chair of the Man Booker Prize judges in 2007, commented that the novel's survival and significance were not in question:

> To read over a hundred novels ... was to step into a fabulous trove of linguistic inventiveness, passion, originality, and energy ...

As McCrum argues in his defence of prizes, the 'final and supreme act of judgement' is one that is immune to media hype or the world of literary lunches: 'it's called reading alone for oneself'.

Book vs Internet

Perhaps the most compelling significance of the popularity of modern writing is the fact that the book, in its conventional form, has survived virtually unchanged as an object since the earliest days of Caxton's printing press. Why? This is an age of unimaginable technological change. John Sutherland, like Robert McCrum, suggests that books survive because reading is, ultimately, not a public matter but an essentially solitary act. Readers do not, apparently, prefer to access books from Google, or download them onto an iPod. Sutherland discusses the unchanging nature of the form, the **codex**, in the chapter 'Every other thing has changed, why hasn't the book changed?'

> What are the features of the codex which have enabled it to survive so long? It is, as I have previously said, a lean-back, not a lean-forward apparatus – and human beings like nothing more than to relax while they read, or spectate ... the codex is wonderfully portable ... More significant is the fact that reading, done well, is ... an act of self-definition. Put another way it is a solitary vice. One reads, as one dreams ... alone.
>
> (*How to Read a Novel: a User's Guide*, 2006)

The American novelist Jane Smiley has also addressed this question of the book as physical object, arguing that books offer delight – and much more:

> An inexpensive book from a reputable publisher is a small, rectangular, boxlike object a few inches long, a few inches wide, and an inch or so thick. It is easy to stack and store, easy to buy, keep, give away, or throw away. As an object, it is user-friendly and routine, a mature technological form, hard to improve upon and easy to like. Many people ... feel better at the mere sight of a book.
> ... The often beautiful cover of a book opens like the lid of a box, but it reveals no objects, rather symbols inscribed on paper. This is simple and elegant, too. The leaves of paper pressed together are reserved and efficient as well as cool and dry. They protect each other from damage. They take up little space. Spread open, they offer some

information, but they don't offer too much, and they don't force it upon [anyone]. They invite perusal. Underneath the open leaves, on either side, are hidden ones that have been read, or remain to be read. The reader may or may not experience them ... Only while the reader is reading does it become a novel.

(*13 Ways of Looking at the Novel*, 2005)

Smiley describes her rapturous pleasure in books: she goes on to claim that her sense of physiological well-being noticeably improves as she looks at the books that have delighted her over years of reading, 'I smile. This row of books elevates my mood.'

Her emphasis is on a world of private pleasure – what some critics have called *jouissance*. But she is also at pains to remind her readers that the novel can have quite different, urgent and profound, functions:

Writing powerfully embodies and develops the will to survive. The Czech novelist Arnošt Lustig was eighteen and had lived in three concentration camps when he escaped from a train heading to Dachau and joined the Czech resistance. His many novels about the Holocaust assert not only his characters' will to survive, but also his own.

The need to write, and the importance of fiction, survives individual and collective horror; Smiley draws attention to the significance of the novel as much-loved object and its value as articulating individual trauma.

The world of Internet fiction, or hyperfiction, proposes a fictional universe in which there is no linear narrative, and no single authorial voice: rather there is a potentially unlimited world of myriad possibilities whereby any 'author' can enter or leave the text at will, rejecting any conventional notion of causality. There can be no eventual outcome; all is provisional, revisable, open-ended. The American critic and novelist Susan Sontag has argued that this negates precisely what we desire in narrative:

A great writer of fiction both *creates* – through acts of imagination, through language that feels inevitable, through vivid forms – a new world, a world that is unique, individual ... Story – the idea that events happen in a specific causal order – is both the way we see the world and what interests us most about it. People who read for nothing else will read for plot.

(quoted in the *Guardian*, March 2007)

▶ How far do you feel that the book will survive developments in technology?

▶ Would you want to read and contribute to narrative fiction online? How does this differ from conventional reading experience?

Is there a modern literary canon?

The literary canon is generally held to be that body of texts which holds undisputed sway in the minds of the majority of critics and educationalists: a core of great works which constitute a literary heritage. The narrowest definition of the fictional canon must be that of the critic F.R. Leavis whose *Great Tradition* (1948) consisted of just some of the novels written by four writers – Jane Austen, George Eliot, Henry James and Joseph Conrad. Since the 1970s, the notion of the 'western canon' has been under attack: too white, too male, too reflective of an elitist cultural world. Feminist critics started to construct alternative canons as a way of drawing attention to women's writing which had been neglected or undiscovered. Today the range of literature studied at both A level and for a degree in English Literature has widened considerably, while the question of the canon will continue to be debated. To discuss the canon, or the texts selected for A-level study, is to become immediately aware that English Literature is a controversial subject.

If you choose to study **gothic** writing at A level or at university, you will encounter, as a matter of course, *Frankenstein, Dracula, Jekyll and Hyde* and, among modern writers, perhaps Angela Carter, Emma Tennant or Patrick McCabe. In other words, the contemporary contribution to the genre is not yet fixed in stone in the way that Mary Shelley or Ann Radcliffe must be. The modern canon is not yet established. Choose to study 'The Victorian Novel' and you would expect to grapple with hefty amounts of Dickens, George Eliot and the Brontës. Students are, of course, encouraged to read outside the canonical texts, but Dickens and Eliot still dominate the centre stage of 'The Victorians'.

Specifying or recommending contemporary texts for academic study is not a simple business: it would be naive to assume that choices are a straightforward matter. Consider two recent winners of the Booker Prize: James Kelman's *How Late It Was, How Late* (1994) and Allan Hollinghurst's *The Line of Beauty* (2004). At the opening of the former, the **protagonist**, Sammy, wakes in a park from a drunken stupor, registers that his shoes have been stolen and almost immediately provokes a fight. When he next comes to consciousness, he is in a police cell and it is gradually dawning on him that he is now blind:

> He was definitely blind but. Fucking weird. Wild. It didnay feel like a nightmare either, that's the funny thing. Even psychologically. In fact it felt okay, an initial wee flurry of excitement but no what ye would call panic-stations. Like it was just a new predicament. Christ it was even making him smile, shaking his head at the very idea, imagining himself telling people; making Helen laugh; she would be as annoyed as fuck but she would still find it funny, eventually, once they had made it up, the stupit fucking row they had had, total misunderstanding man but it was fine now, it would be fine once she saw him.

> Now he was chuckling away to himself. How the hell was it
> happening to him! It's no as if he was ear-marked for glory!
> Even in practical terms, once the nonsense passed, he started
> thinking about it; this was a new stage in life, a development. A new
> epoch!

The narrative is conveyed through Sammy's Glaswegian interior monologue or through direct speech. In the novel the direct speech is famously known for its repeated use of 'swear-words' and it has been observed that response to the novel became dominated by this: reviewers 'unable accurately to recount the plot of the novel could tell you precisely how many times the [word] "fuck" ... appear in its pages'. Simon Jenkins in *The Times* described the author, rather than the protagonist, as 'an illiterate savage'. Geoff Gilbert, analysing Kelman's work in Rod Mengham's *An Introduction to Contemporary Fiction* (1999), argues that swearing operates on three levels in the text: 'a realist swearing, operating between characters in the novel; the way that swear words regulate a heightened intensity at certain moments of the prose ... and the way that swearing informs a reductive but uneasy characterisation of the novel in debates that surrounded the Booker Prize'. Kelman's text was judged by some readers to be unacceptable because of its language. The subject matter of the novel or the character of the protagonist seemed irrelevant to the debate.

Irvine Welsh in *Trainspotting* (1993) writes with splenetic rage, his style a furious explosion of hatred and defiance. Here too, the reprinted text challenges the potential reader (or purchaser) to consider the book as 'a seminal novel that changed the face of British fiction' (Vintage Books, 2004). So, have we attained a liberal consensus where anything can be published and we do not recoil from what was once unprintable? John Mullan, discussing Mark Haddon's *The Curious Incident of the Dog in the Night-Time* (2003), refers to complaints that the use of swearing is unsuited to 'young readers' – one reader 'even recruited their MP to complain' (*How Novels Work*, 2006). Clearly, language remains a problematic area.

In Hollinghurst's novel, the 'line of beauty' of the title refers in part to the proposed title for an artistic magazine – *'Ogee'* – where it denotes a curved shape in architecture. It is also the line of cocaine, which fuels the social lives of the febrile personalities of the text. Set in the aggressive world of 1980s Thatcherism, the protagonist here is an Oxford graduate, living amongst the moneyed and privileged world of Notting Hill, and pursuing his first gay love affairs against a background of right-wing homophobia and the earliest awareness of AIDS. The text is as sexually explicit as Kelman's is colloquial:

> ... a line wasn't feasibly resisted. He loved the etiquette of the thing,
> the chopping with a credit card, the passing of the tightly rolled note,

the procedure courteous and dry, 'all done with money', as Wani
said – it was part of the larger beguilement, and once it had begun it
squeezed him with its charm and promise. Being careful not to nudge
him as he worked, he hugged Wani lightly from behind and slid a
hand into his left trouser pocket.

One of the invigorating aspects of studying contemporary fiction is precisely the
lack of canonicity. The arbitrariness of textual choice has always existed: there are
authors and texts that transcend the fashion of the moment and there are writers
whose fame simply evaporates. In the past, A-level texts have included such titles as
The Knight of the Burning Pestle, *Eothen*, *Sohrab and Rustum* – but few students
have heard of them today. Whether the choices of 2008 will still be read in ten,
twenty or fifty years, we cannot know. In a world of constantly changing literary
trends, we select what we deem worthwhile – now.

The history of the novel is one which reminds us that there are texts which
continue to be relished and enjoyed across different periods, and there are texts
which have been banned or denounced at different times. Such texts we now read
as a matter of course, without necessarily recoiling at the content but curious
about the cultural world which has sought to deny them to readers.

▶ Would you exclude certain texts from academic study? What is your own view of an
author's use of controversial language?

Contemporary novel, contemporary life?

… the novelist [is] a person who performs a function essential to the
soul of every community: the secret conscience of the tribe.
(Colm Tóibín and Carmen Callil *The Modern Library:
the 200 Best Novels in English Since 1950*, 1999)

… 'the everyday' [is] not merely ennui, pointlessness, repetition,
triviality; it is beauty as well …
(Milan Kundera *The Curtain*, 2007)

Is the principal duty of contemporary writing to portray the society we inhabit?
Do novelists seek to explore the complexities of modern society? To what extent
does the contemporary novelist assume the prophetic role of Charles Dickens and
become a social commentator?

When a writer – be it Dickens or McEwan – chooses to locate his writing within
the empirical, urban world, he does so for a purpose. He is offering his readers a
recognisable portrait of their society and can thereby draw the readers' attention
to facts they have not observed or acknowledged; he can confront and challenge
expectations or prejudices. He might, ultimately, offer resolutions to perceived

anxieties. There will be a unique relationship with the reader; indeed reviewers of current novels sometimes express the extent to which they would quarrel with or reject the novelist's vision. It could be argued that it is in the depiction of the everyday world that the writer might be most controversial. This is certainly true of writers such as J.M. Coetzee, whose novels of South Africa illustrate the complexities and difficulties of post-apartheid society. (The different uses of narrative realism are discussed in detail in Part 2.)

Perhaps the single fact to be emphasised here would be the pluralism of modern society and the corresponding range of its fictions. The 'contemporary' is often far from simple: fictional writing in the English language now extends across many borders. Again, the prize world is helpful in demonstrating the extent to which 'the English novel' has become 'the novel in Britain'. Richard Todd, in *Consuming Fictions: The Booker Prize and Fiction in Britain Today* (1996), states that the 'catchment area' of the Booker comprises one quarter of the world's population. In other words, 'the novel in Britain' now includes fiction from Australia, New Zealand, Canada, South Africa, Nigeria, the Caribbean, as well as other areas of the world, but published in Britain. Contemporary Scottish and Irish writers, whether or not asserting their non-Englishness, also fall into this category. It is precisely this plurality which has saved the novel from extinction: when *Granta* debated 'The end of the English Novel' in 1980, it was the 'Englishness' of the genre which attracted particular criticism. Frederick Bowers, writing from an American perspective, defined this as 'Irrelevant Parochialism':

> What strikes an expatriate most about the contemporary British novel is its conformity, its traditional sameness, and its realistically rendered provincialism. Shaped only by its contents, the British novel is the product of group mentality: local, quaint, and self-consciously xenophobic.

What emerges from the debates about the genre which proliferated towards the end of the 20th century is that the post-war English novel suffered acute myopia and timidity: it 'appeared to be strangling in its own decorous and unappetising repressions', as academic writer Lorna Sage described in *Granta*. It is then revitalised by new voices and perspectives:

> ... much of what's significant in English fiction is written with 'elsewhere' very much in mind; is, in a sense, written *from* elsewhere.

In other words, one of the aspects of the novel which has changed most in recent years is that, whereas Dickens described his world from his own perspective within that world, the contemporary novelists who evoke London life (including Monica Ali, Zadie Smith, Hanif Kureishi) are writers whose perspective comes in part from 'elsewhere'.

▶ Think about the quotation from Milan Kundera above, and relate it to any novel you feel to be rooted in 'the everyday'. Has the novelist revealed the beauty, as well as the triviality, of modern life?

Cultural hybridity and identity

In a strictly geographical sense, the British novel could be said to be any work of fiction written by an English, Welsh, Scottish or Northern Irish writer. But must that writer be born here? Of British parents? Could 'English fiction' be any novel written in the English language, regardless of the passport(s) of the author? One of the reasons for the end-of-century exuberance in fiction must be the creative energy supplied by writers with differing perspectives on the question of 'Britishness'. Equally, the theme of identity itself is one particularly suited to the novel. It is certainly the case that courses entitled 'The Modern Novel' will include 'Post-colonialism' as a subject to be explored through its fictions; indeed it often constitutes a discrete topic for study. But 'multiculturalism' may already be a term passing its sell-by date. Philip Tew, academic writer on the modern novel, observes that

> ... a determined effort to read texts in terms of gender, ethnicity, post-coloniality and radical issues ... ended in ghettoising or marginalising such creative efforts in thematic studies of these issues. Like so much critical practice it raises some awareness, but its appropriateness diminishes as cultural acceptance of such voices broadens, since their very separation as separable categories ... maintains the dynamics of the too knowing categorisations of oppression.
>
> (*The Contemporary British Novel*, 2004)

Philip Tew is arguing that Zadie Smith, for example, should not be considered as a 'marginalised' voice. To do so would be patronising or simply risible. Undoubtedly, the novel is the genre best placed to explore the complexities of change and its implications. The Marxist critic Terry Eagleton, in *After Theory* (2003), comments that the subject of the novel was once class struggle – 'now embarrassingly passé' – but that the compelling subject has now become the exploration of cultural identity. The academic and critic Brian Shaffer argues that the novel is, *par excellence*:

> ... [the] open-ended, socially-engaged, exploratory genre, one that challenges and stretches the canons of knowledge (the 'conventional wisdom') as well as the prevailing standards of perception, subjectivity and literary representation in its bid to picture and probe an evolving contemporary reality.
>
> (*Reading the Novel in English 1950–2000*, 2006)

The complex nature of these realities can be illustrated by considering the 'identities' of three well-established writers: Zadie Smith, born in London of a Jamaican mother and English father; Kazuo Ishiguro, born in Japan, educated in England; and Hanif Kureishi, English and Indian, caught between the working-class life of his school friends in Bromley and the privileged background of his father's family in Pakistan. Kureishi writes of the experience of alienation in his south London world; Zadie Smith in *White Teeth* (2000) satirises the liberal, middle-class acknowledgement of 'multiculturalism'. In the following quotation, Samad Iqbal – parent governor at his children's school – has questioned whether the school's Harvest Festival is pagan. The headmistress explains their policy:

> 'Mr Iqbal, we have been through the matter of religious festivals quite thoroughly in the autumn review. As I am sure you are aware, the school already recognises a great variety of religious and secular events: amongst them, Christmas, Ramadan, Chinese New Year, Diwali, Yom Kippur, Hanukkah, the birthday of Haile Selassie, and the death of Martin Luther King. The Harvest Festival is part of the school's ongoing commitment to religious diversity, Mr Iqbal.'

How far, then, might hybridity be taken as a rule rather than an exception?

Peter Childs suggests that British contemporary fiction provides a new geographical perspective, co-existing with, but different from, Europe and the United States: that of Britain's imperial past and post-colonial present, whereby writers such as Rushdie, Smith, Kureishi

> … depict an 'in-between' experience and viewpoint in their novels, aware of the changes needed to be wrought on traditional ideas of British identity in order to include the migrant's experience and also recognise the new British ethnic mix brought about by the post-war diaspora.
>
> (*Contemporary Novelists*, 2005)

This is the territory explored in the writing of Andrea Levy in *Small Island* (2004) and Monica Ali in *Brick Lane* (2005).

There is a world of difference between the comic parody of *White Teeth* and Khaled Hosseini's *The Kite Runner* (2003), where the question of identity is both inescapable and painful. In *The Kite Runner,* the **narrator** has spent his adult life in America, where he remains haunted by the violence and betrayals from his childhood in Afghanistan. He returns, eventually, to Kabul to witness the fundamentalist brutality of the Taliban and to rescue the child of his former playmate, Hassan. Here, identity is complicated by the weight of history: Hassan and his family have always known persecution because, as members of the Hazara ethnic group, they are considered inferior. But the novel has concealed secrets which are not discovered until the conclusion of the text. The narrator struggles to reconcile his American life with his Afghan past, but must also accommodate truths about himself and his father that he had not anticipated.

Anne Tyler's *Digging to America* (2006) is a subtle and probing exploration of individual and national identity. Here, two Korean baby girls arrive in Baltimore/ Washington Airport on the night of Friday 15th August 1997, to be adopted into two very different American families. The Dickinson-Donaldsons (Bitsy and Brad) are born and bred in Baltimore; they will offer their daughter Jin-Ho a devoted American family life, while also scrupulously attempting to maintain a sense of Korean identity for her, reading her Korean folk-tales, for example, and dressing her in traditional costume for festive events. The Zazdan family (Ziba and Sami) are Iranian-American, part of a large extended family which settled in the USA following the 1979 revolution and the overthrow of the Shah. Ziba and Sami are an entirely integrated couple who have grown up in Baltimore and are happy to introduce their daughter, Susan, to an American way of life, although they maintain the cultural traditions of their respective Iranian families. A degree of satiric comedy arises from the different attitudes and expectations of the two couples to their daughters. A sharper, more critical perspective is offered by Sami's mother, Maryam, who has been an American citizen for thirty-nine years, yet still feels that she is 'forever a guest, on her very best behaviour'. She, alone, can say, 'I was so sad to become American'. The novel constantly returns to the theme of immigration as Tyler uses the annual 'Arrival Party' as a means of structuring her material. An intriguing insight into the possible advantages of being the newcomer is offered at one of these parties; a perspective notably lacking from recent British novels of immigrant communities, such as *White Teeth*, *Brick Lane* and *Small Island*:

> One day not too far off, immigrants are going to be the new elite in this country. That's because they bear no burden of guilt. Their forefathers didn't steal any Native American land and they never owned slaves. They have perfectly clear consciences.

The Kite Runner does depict the protagonist's successful integration into American life, but Hosseini also suggests that the weight of past tragedy can never be overcome. Tyler seems to imply that the future for the two adoptees is the brightest one, free from the history of their origins and apart from the history of their adopted country. Kiran Desai's *The Inheritance of Loss* (2006), by way of comparison, describes an entirely negative experience of immigrant life in America: the young Biju is employed as slave labour in appalling conditions and his dream of freedom and prosperity has to be abandoned.

▶ Thinking about the quotation from *Digging to America*, above, look at the extract from *Small Island* in Part 3 (page 88) and compare attitudes to immigration and the place of the newcomer.

Politics and the novel: 'Thatcherism'

'Thatcherism' is a term that needs to be placed in inverted commas to indicate its complexity: it denotes a period of late 20th-century history and the right-wing political ideology associated with that time; it also connotes the way in which a cultural opposition to that ideology found expression in the arts. In May 1979, Margaret Thatcher, the newly elected Conservative Prime Minister, announced her intention of reversing the direction of post-war consensus politics in favour of a radical new agenda of economic and social change. In terms of the macro-economic, this meant the privatisation of nationalised industries and the steady dismantling of Britain's industrial and manufacturing heartlands: the emphasis was to be shifted to the free-market and consumer demand. Individual pursuit of wealth was fostered by changes in taxation. Famously, Thatcher declared in 1987, 'there is no such thing as society' – a clarion call to encourage private or family ambition, at the expense of moral concern for society as a whole. Rising unemployment, accompanied by restrictions on trades' union activity, led to violent clashes in the miners' strikes of 1984, and there were riots in a number of deprived areas of major cities – scenes unparalleled in British 20th-century history.

An awareness of a divided nation emerged: the devastation and hopelessness of traditional industrial communities of the north where unemployment and poverty were endemic, compared with conspicuous consumerism and ostentation in areas of the south-east. This was the world featured in films such as *Billy Elliot* (2000), *The Full Monty* (1997) or in Ian McEwan's filmscript *The Ploughman's Lunch* (1983). The Conservative government also sought to change 'permissive' social attitudes with legislation such as Clause 28 which outlawed 'positive' gay and lesbian images in schools. Internationally, Thatcher sought to identify with right-wing President Ronald Reagan in the USA, distancing herself from the European alliance, and endorsing Reagan's cold-war policies by welcoming American nuclear weapons in England.

The arts in opposition

Fiction flourished in this period. Historically, the arts have often opposed the status quo and the novel is a genre with immense satiric potential. At a time when financial support for higher education and for the arts was subject to government cuts, radicalism in the arts became a thriving concern. The role of the novel in defining a *Zeitgeist* (characteristic mood of the times) is complex: Steven Connor suggests that it is 'not just as passively marked with the imprint of history, but also as one of the ways in which history is made and remade' (*The English Novel in History, 1950 to 1995*, 1996). The novel is itself an agent of perception and changing opinion; it doesn't simply record.

Martin Amis incarnates the spirit of the Thatcherite 1980s in John Self, the protagonist of *Money* (1984), a ruthless advertising executive who is addicted to 'swearing, fighting, hitting women, smoking, drinking, fast food, pornography, gambling and hand-jobs'. Ian McEwan's *Amsterdam* (1998) is a black comedy which satirises the sleaze and hypocrisy which, for McEwan, characterised the latter years of the Conservative Party in government. In Jonathan Coe's *What a Carve Up!* (1994), the personalities of an entire family dynasty exemplify different aspects of Conservative policies internationally, financially, agriculturally and politically. Mark, for example, sells arms to Iraq, protected in part by his politician cousin Henry and right-wing journalist sister, Hilary. Dorothy is discovering ways in which factory farming can create maximum profit.

London has been a compelling theme for many writers of the English novel, from its inception in the early 18th century and Defoe's *Moll Flanders* through to the teeming and predatory world of Dickens. There are many 20th-century writers, conscious of this heritage, who sought an imaginative expression of the decay and despair of the city. In *London: A Social History* (1994), Roy Porter discussed the way in which London appeared to decline into a 'third world' city:

> Homelessness – eradicated by the mid twentieth century – became endemic again in the Thatcher years. Swarms of dossers and vagrants appeared, cardboard cities sprouting in the luxuriance of yuppie affluence. An encampment of tramps and the homeless arose at the Waterloo Bridge roundabout, fifty yards from the Festival of Britain site and next to the National Theatre, while elegant Lincoln's Inn Fields became a Third World shanty town for scores of the homeless – a settlement tolerated for several years, since nobody wished to assume responsibility. As in Third World countries, thousands in London now beg by day … and sleep rough in shop doorways and church porches.

London continues to play an important role in the fictional writing of the post-Thatcher period: McEwan's *Saturday* (2006) and Graham Swift's *The Light of Day* (2003) both take place within one day in London streets that are described with complete geographical accuracy; Zadie Smith's *White Teeth* and Monica Ali's *Brick Lane* draw upon specific locations within London. In the latter text, Nazneen has moved from her Bangladeshi village to Tower Hamlets and a tower block inappropriately named 'Rosemead'. Here she contemplates the 'dead grass and broken paving stones' she sees from her window:

> The sun is large and sickly. It sweats uncomfortably in a hazy sky, squeezed in between slabs of concrete. There is barely enough sky to

hold it. Below, the communal bins ring the courtyard like squat metal warriors, competing in foulness, contemplating the stand-off. One has keeled over and spilled its guts. A rat flicks in and out of them.

In terms of the politics of the late 20th century, Hollinghurst's *Line of Beauty* is concerned to display the moneyed Thatcherite world of the 1980s, with its cocaine-fuelled parties, while Irvine Welsh's *Trainspotting* reveals the obverse side of the coin in both London and Edinburgh with the alcohol and heroin addiction of a predatory underclass. Iain Sinclair is perhaps *the* chronicler of contemporary London with a series of fictional and non-fictional books, including *White Chappell, Scarlet Tracings* (1987) and *Downriver* (1991), which travel the capital city charting its chaos and decay.

Salman Rushdie: the continuing controversy

One of the enduring ironies of the end of the Thatcher era, in terms of publishing and the novel, must be the situation of Salman Rushdie. In 1981 he won the Booker Prize with *Midnight's Children*. Richard Todd reflected the weight of contemporary critical opinion when he observed in his study of the Booker Prize in 1996 that it was a book which changed 'for ever the way a British readership looked back on its colonial past'. It was also selected as the 'Booker of Bookers' in 1993 to mark the 25th anniversary of the award. *The Satanic Verses* (1988) almost immediately aroused controversy in Britain and internationally for its apparent disrespect for Islam – although the main theme of the book was the fragmentation and incoherence of a Britain ruled by a 'Mrs Torture'. Extraordinary scenes of book-burnings and riots followed the publication of *The Satanic Verses* and Iran's Ayatollah Khomeini pronounced a *fatwa*, a death sentence on Rushdie, for blasphemy. This *fatwa* cannot be revoked, although the threat to Rushdie is now perceived as diminished. However, Rushdie's Japanese translator was murdered and his Italian translator wounded, and a number of bookstores around the world were fire-bombed for stocking the novel. Rushdie was forced into hiding, living a life dependent on the British security forces for some years. He had opposed the authoritarian 'fundamentalism' of Margaret Thatcher, yet required its armed vigilance for his personal safety. In June 2007 Rushdie was awarded a knighthood in the Queen's Birthday Honours' List, to mark his exceptional achievement in literature. This reignited the controversy surrounding *The Satanic Verses* and caused diplomatic difficulties with countries who still regarded Rushdie as a hated figure. Rushdie himself was again threatened with assassination and some people continue to see the politics of the novel as dangerous.

For the first time in modern British history, a writer of fiction was in danger of his life for an imaginative work, for a novel generally regarded as part of a tradition of **magic realism**: a genre which would seem to resist literal-minded protest. At the opening of the novel, characters fall, apparently unharmed, from a plane; yet the substance of this text was considered sacrilegious and inflammatory. Rushdie's own claims for the importance of the novel are crucial:

> I am not trying to say that *The Satanic Verses* is 'only a novel' … Those who oppose the novel most vociferously today are of the opinion that intermingling with a different culture will inevitably weaken and ruin their own. I am of the opposite opinion. *The Satanic Verses* celebrates hybridity, impurity, intermingling … It rejoices in mongrelisation and fears the absolutism of the Pure.
>
> (*Imaginary Homelands*, 1991)

▶ Think of a novel which might seem politically sensitive (examples cited include Coetzee's *Disgrace*, Khaled Hosseini's *The Kite Runner*). Discuss the treatment of political tension or conflict in the text. Does the novel suggest the possibility of resolution?

Literature and taboo: the relish of the nasty

Any discussion of the controversies provoked by contemporary arts and the literary canon introduces, naturally, the notion of the writer's conscious desire to shock and repel the reader. Just as Tarantino's films *Reservoir Dogs* (1992) and *Pulp Fiction* (1994) gained a cult following in the 1990s, so the novel has also sought to challenge and provoke with evocations of extreme brutality or the delineation of a profoundly disturbed psyche. Indeed, it could be argued that it is a feature of the *fin-de-siècle* text to do so, just as in the 1890s *Dracula* played upon the cultural anxieties of its time as well as suggesting startling sexual perversions and acts of violence. Why does post-1990 writing challenge readers with extreme and troubling subject matter? Academic critic Linden Peach discusses the way in which novelists pursue taboo to the limit, suggesting that late 20th-century writing is preoccupied with 'exhaustion, excess, limit and transgression' (*The Contemporary Irish Novel*, 2004). He uses the ideas of French philosopher Michel Foucault (1926–1984), who questioned whether the 20th century had shown any progress, seeing it rather as the period which witnessed 'the death of God' and therefore also the death of meaning.

One of the obvious areas in which novelists play with ideas of taboo and transgression is the gothic, a genre which has continued to flourish in contemporary writing. The Irish writer Patrick McCabe uses the dark world of the gothic to introduce the forbidden theme of paedophilia in the Catholic Church. He explores psychotic states of alienation and madness in *The Dead School* (1995) and *The Butcher Boy* (1992). In both of these texts there is clearly a desire to pursue disturbing subjects to the limit, to the extent that the reader is in an ambivalent relationship with the writing, both intellectually engaged yet repelled. In *The Butcher Boy*, the child Francie has been abused by his priest and told by his neighbour, Mrs Nugent, that he is a pig. The novel is narrated retrospectively by Francie and the reader remains uncertain as to the veracity of his delusional world; he recounts a horrifying identification with pigs and a gruesome revenge upon Mrs Nugent. How much of his bleak narrative is factual and how much imagined? In *The Dead School*, McCabe charts the total disintegration of Raphael Bell, the headmaster of a notable school in Dublin. When he is forced to resign, Bell creates his own macabre Dead School in his home. Remote, finally, from every restraint of his previously disciplined and pious existence, he pursues a deranged course of self-destruction until he is finally discovered, hanging in the wreckage of his once serene and entirely proper home.

Nowadays, an interesting aspect of the inevitable controversy arising from such writing is the way in which books have been marketed to include hostile criticism as part of the **paratext** of the novel. Iain Banks' *The Wasp Factory*, when reprinted in paperback form, included as part of the blurb before the text:

> 'It is a sick, sick, world when the confidence and investment of an astute firm of publishers is justified by a work of unparalleled depravity.' *Irish Times*

> 'As a piece of writing, *The Wasp Factory* soars to the level of mediocrity. Maybe the crassly explicit language, the obscenity of the plot, were thought to strike an agreeably avant-garde note. Perhaps it is all a joke, meant to fool literary London into respect for rubbish.' *The Times*

Yet it is also hailed as a 'minor masterpiece' and Selina Hastings, reviewing the novel in the *Daily Telegraph*, declared that '[Banks'] study of an obsessive personality is extraordinary, written with a clarity and attention to detail that is most impressive'. The intention here is to involve the reader in the unresolved debate that is presented. Here is a work of unusual barbarism and bizarre sadism: it is up to the reader to decide whether it justifies the praise or abuse.

Kiernan Ryan, in his discussion of 'Sex, Violence and Complicity: Martin Amis and Ian McEwan' (in Rod Mengham [ed.] *An Introduction to Contemporary Fiction*, 1999), identifies Amis'

> ... exuberant immersion in the cheap, cruel world that he has conjured up. The suspicion is that Amis relishes being nasty. He seems to delight in investing the subhuman and vicious, the mean and degenerate, with a charismatic energy and turbo-charged eloquence which sanction and protract their modern sway.

Indeed, Amis is willing to concede a 'sort of horrible Dickensian glee' in delineating horrific tortures for his protagonists. Equally, as Ryan observes, McEwan is widely perceived as 'a novelist obsessed with the perverted, the depraved and the macabre, an inscrutable voyeur who describes abjection and obscenity with chilling detachment'. Readers are alienated by McEwan's 'refusal to act as decency demands to the shocking scenes staged by his own morbid imagination'. In other words, there is a repugnance engendered by the subject matter of McEwan's work (in particular, his early writing) but there is also an objection to the detachment of his prose style. Amis repels his readers differently: for his seeming delight in the sordid brutalities of his protagonists.

Two questions emerge from this *fin-de-siècle* pursuit of the grotesque and morbid. First, does the subject matter derive from alienation with the cultural context of the writer – has a repugnance for the brutal realities of everyday existence provoked these fictional extremes by way of reaction? *Trainspotting* is a novel about nihilism and desensitisation: how can this be conveyed other than through the text's seeming indifference to the degradations and violence delineated? Second, is subject matter unconnected with context, deriving rather from an experimentalism with language and with the genre itself: simply a narrative questioning of 'how far can you go'? Again, there are commercial implications: can anything be published and sold?

There has also been a tendency for late 20th-century writers to take advantage of liberal publishing attitudes to produce shocking and disturbing writing in order to convey something of the reality of extreme experiences of the past. The Holocaust is perhaps the obvious example of this, as is any writing engaging directly with the slaughter and suffering of warfare. Style is a means by which the author can affect the reader: in Toni Morrison's *Beloved* (1987), language can be densely lyrical and poetic but it can also be horrifyingly direct. In Morrison's writing style is a way of challenging the complacencies of her American reader. She wishes to convey a numinous other-worldliness which derives from mystical African roots and she also wishes to unsettle her readers with the stark truths of slavery.

Pat Barker's novels are unsparing in their evocation of trench warfare: from the beginning of *Regeneration* (1991), the novel questions what, in the context of unremitting everyday barbarism, can possibly be regarded as normal or sane. The language is brutal because the events are aberrant. The novel confronts the loss of individual voices – men who cannot speak because the trauma of their experiences has frozen their ability to articulate – and acknowledges the inadequacy of verbal communication:

> Language ran out on you, in the end, the names were left to say it all.
> Mons, Loos, Ypres, the Somme. Arras.

▶ 'Style is a writer's way of telling the truth.' (Zadie Smith, *Guardian*, 13 January 2007) How has any text you have studied used language in a way which challenges the reader? Have you found this effective?

Biographical fictions

It might, justifiably, seem that the modern novel has unlimited creative freedom. The previous section offers some examination of ways in which different writers have challenged thematic and linguistic limits. It is intriguing, then, that this has also proved a period in which a number of novelists have chosen other works of literature, or the lives of previous writers, as fictional subjects. In 2004, by bizarre coincidence, three novels inspired by the life of the writer Henry James appeared: David Lodge's *Author, Author*, Colm Tóibín's *The Master* and Alan Hollinghurst's *The Line of Beauty*. In terms of genre this is not a unique phenomenon: other writers have recently based novels on Dostoevsky, Samuel Johnson, Sylvia Plath, R.L. Stevenson, Keats, Sir Arthur Conan Doyle, to cite just a few. David Lodge, academic and critic, as well as novelist, defines this type of writing:

> The biographical novel … takes a real person and their real history as the subject matter for imaginative exploration, using the novel's techniques for representing subjectivity rather than the objective, evidence-based discourse of biography.
>
> (*The Year of Henry James*, 2006)

It is perhaps the combination of the 'real' with the imaginative that has proved compelling to novelists. In common with historical writing, the drama and excitement of real events can be evoked, yet the novelist can still operate with considerable licence. It may be the quality of difference between contemporary life and a given historical moment that inspires the writer's engagement.

Penelope Fitzgerald's *The Blue Flower* (1996) is a concise yet intricately detailed account of the brief period of early German Romanticism, during which the young poet Friedrich von Hardenberg (known later as Novalis) became totally infatuated with the adolescent Sophie Kuhn. The **epigraph** to the novel, a quotation from Novalis, draws attention to the artist's perception of the dichotomy between different types of writing: 'Novels arise out of the shortcomings of history.' The statement could be taken to allude to both Novalis as a Romantic poet and prose writer, and to Fitzgerald herself, writing at the end of the 20th century. The creative artist will always perceive the world of empirical fact as limiting. On the one hand, *The Blue Flower* is a novel which relishes the physical actuality of Novalis' world, that of 1790s Saxony. The reader learns much about the domestic arrangements of the family: the laundry; the soups of beer, sugar and eggs; rose-hips and onions; bread and cabbage-water; cows' udders with nutmeg. Within this dense physical detail, the central fact of Novalis' idealised passion for Sophie remains mysterious. She is no more than a twelve-year-old child when he first meets her, largely uneducated and with few ideas beyond the enjoyment of the moment. Yet, to the poet she is 'my true Philosophy ... my spirit's guide in all things', offering glimpses of immortality itself. The writing of Novalis echoes throughout the novel, in particular the central symbol of an unfinished prose work, *Heinrich von Ofterdingen*, the story of a young man who experiences 'unspeakable longings ... to see the blue flower'. This yearning for the transcendent characterises the sensibility of Romanticism itself and infuses Novalis' vision of life. His love for Sophie is presented as mysterious: neither his family nor friends can see beyond the 'decent, good-hearted Saxon girl, potato fed'. And the love affair is doomed as Sophie is already ill with tuberculosis when she consents, at thirteen, to marry Novalis. Although their engagement is formalised, she dies two days after her fifteenth birthday, in March 1797, Novalis himself only surviving her by four years. Fitzgerald unites in this work a brief and tragic love story, poignant for its biographical truth, with the seasonal housekeeping world of central Germany. She captures a fleeting moment of absolute intensity, within the emotional life of one individual and within the dominant literary movement of Europe.

In *Arthur and George* (2005), Julian Barnes engages with England at a particular Edwardian moment when the great man of letters, Sir Arthur Conan Doyle, and a quietly self-effacing vicarage son, George Edalji, meet to clear the latter's name from criminal conviction. Both men are historical personages and the disputed case is also factual, revealing much about the society and politics of the day. The novel juxtaposes the lives of the two men to reveal their different attitudes and ambitions; the extent to which their individual lives harmonise with the dominant ethos of their day – or challenge it. George is half-Parsee and as such struggles to be acknowledged in the light of prejudice and ignorance. Barnes is interested in playing upon the idea of fictionality itself – Conan Doyle is called upon to act the part of his own invention, Sherlock Holmes. Indeed, various characters clearly confuse the author with his creation. So the novel interweaves different layers of fact and fiction to attempt to arrive at a resolution which could satisfactorily be 'truth'. One of the aspects of the novel which anchors it firmly in its historical moment is Conan Doyle's profound belief in the prevailing fashion for spiritualism and clairvoyance. The novel concludes in 1930, but in its description of a packed Albert Hall waiting to hear the clairvoyant revelations of the famous medium Mrs Roberts, it seems as remote as the medieval Catholicism of Unsworth's *Morality Play* (see Part 3, page 100).

Why, then, have recent writers chosen to base fictional works on other writers? David Lodge suggests that there are several possible answers:

It could be taken as a symptom of a declining faith or loss of confidence in the power of purely fictional narrative, in a culture where we are bombarded from every direction with factual narrative in the form of 'news'. It could be regarded as a characteristic move of postmodernism – incorporating the art of the past in its own processes through reinterpretation and stylistic pastiche. It could be seen as a sign of decadence and exhaustion in contemporary writing, or as positive and ingenious ...

(*The Year of Henry James*, 2006)

Lodge offers a wide range of interpretation here – from the bleak possibility that the novel has become a somewhat tired genre, in need of transfusion of new ideas from the past, through a notion of the novel as essentially playful and experimental, to the possibility of the novel's ability to reinvent itself and find new inspiration.

▶ Think about the epigraph to *The Blue Flower* quoted earlier: 'Novels arise out of the shortcomings of history.' What are the advantages of the novel as a form in terms of historical or biographical material?

The British novel and war writing

'The parapet, the wire, and the mud [are now] permanent features of human existence.' Which is to say that anxiety without end, without purpose, without reward, and without meaning is woven into the fabric of contemporary life.

(Paul Fussell *The Great War and Modern Memory*, 1975)

The end of the 20th century has seen some fine historically based fictions: writers such as Barry Unsworth, Peter Ackroyd, Matthew Kneale and Adam Thorpe have all chosen to set novels in other times, sometimes choosing a subject redolent with crisis, such as the slave trade (Unsworth, *Sacred Hunger*, 1992), at other times evoking a historical perspective to create an imaginatively compelling world of difference. One of the fictional motifs that recurs insistently at the end of the 20th century is the catastrophic warfare that has marked the period. The First World War is the subject of Pat Barker's *Regeneration* trilogy (*Regeneration*, 1991; *The Eye in the Door*, 1993; *The Ghost Road*, 1995) and Sebastian Faulks's *Birdsong* (1993). The Second World War supplies the context for Michael Ondaatje's *The English Patient* (1992), Michael Frayn's *Spies* (2002), Rachel Seiffert's *The Dark Room* (2001), Louis de Bernières' *Captain Corelli's Mandolin* (1994) and Sarah Waters' *The Night Watch* (2006). And there is no shortage of such works in translation into English, the writing of W.G. Sebald being particularly significant.

The key question here must be why fictional writers choose to revisit these scenes of conflict from a much later perspective, indeed as essentially post-war writers. The writer George Steiner offers a compelling explanation: he identifies the 'political bestiality' of the mid-20th century as erupting within western civilisation itself:

> [Barbarism] did not spring up in the Gobi desert or the rain forests of the Amazon. It rose from within, and from the core of European civilisation. The cry of the murdered sounded in earshot of the universities; the sadism went on a street away from the theatres and museums … In our own day the high places of literacy, of philosophy, of artistic expression, became the setting for Belsen.
>
> (*Language and Silence*, 1967)

Equally, circumstances of an exceptional kind are morally and emotionally compelling to the imaginative writer, and to readers. The intensity of such experiences produces euphoria as well as fear. In his post-9/11 novel *The Good Life*, Jay McInerney selects as an epigraph to the text, a quotation from Ana Menendez (a Cuban-American writer):

> Cataclysmic events, whatever their outcome, are as rare and transporting as a great love. Bombings, revolutions, earthquakes, hurricanes – anyone who has passed through one and lived, if they are honest, will tell you that even in the depths of their fear, there was an exhilaration such as had been missing from their lives until then.

In wartime fictions the 'normal' boundaries of class, religion and decorum are in abeyance. They might prove to have value – or not. There can be no ready assumptions. Clearly, we are not, as readers, being invited to empathise with the everyday. We are not seeking the familiar; rather we are confronted with trauma and incomprehension. The soldiers treated by the coldly brutal Dr Yelland in Barker's *Regeneration* have responded by retreating into silence – for which they will be punished. One of the historical reasons for this proliferation of material is the inevitable disappearance of the authentic voices of the period: at the end of the 20th century only a few First World War survivors were still able to speak of their experiences; a number of historical projects around the country seek to commit the memories of Second World War combatants to permanent record. An urgent sense that a certain historical voice is nearly extinct might be one of the reasons to approach the subject through fiction. In Barker's *Another World* (1998), the fictional Geordie is still preoccupied at the end of his life with his wartime experiences:

> … in the 1960s, Geordie began to talk about the war. Over the next three decades his willingness to share his memories increased and, as other veterans died around him, his own rarity value grew. In the 1990s he was one of a tiny group of survivors who gathered for the

anniversaries of the first day of the Somme, and most of the others were in wheelchairs. There were rewards for him in this. He was sought after, listened to, he had friends, interests, a purpose in life at an age when old people are too often sitting alone in chilly rooms waiting for their relatives to phone.

Memory itself is the subject here: individual memory and society's collective memory – and the question of whether one is privileged over the other. Barker's characters dwell on the fact of memory: the historian of *Another World*, Helen, believes that traumatic memories are first repressed, then altered in order to merge with society's collective account of traumatic experience. But, for Geordie, memory operates in different ways: in part, with a sense of collective responsibility. He wants to warn his grandson's world that '*It happened once, therefore it can happen again. Take care.*' His own private memories are both persistent and unresolved: he remains haunted to the end of his long life by a sense of guilt over the death of his brother. At the age of 101, dying of cancer, Geordie believes that it is his bayonet wound which pains and is destroying him. The historian cannot grasp this although Nick, the grandson, can: 'Geordie's past isn't over. It isn't even the past.'

Steven Connor suggests that one of the effects of history in the novel can be to

> … bring about psychological and cultural *enlargement*. Narrative can lengthen memory or extend forethought, in the elaboration of the past and extrapolation into possible futures.
>
> (*The English Novel in History 1950 to 1995*, 1996)

Pat Barker's writing is particularly successful in this concept of 'enlargement'. Because her *Regeneration* trilogy merges historical and fictional characters, it pays tribute to 'memory' while also assuming the novelist's right to invent. Thus the 'memory' of Sassoon might be real or invented. Both are equally possible. Just as the tortured individuals in Craiglockhart Hospital are trapped in unimaginable memories, Barker is also implying that British society is trapped in certain patterns of historical memory which she seeks to challenge. Her stated view of history is that it is a 'trauma that needs to be worked through'. In that case, literature is a form of exorcism or expiation. The inclusion of Sassoon, in particular, emphasises the way in which our later perception of the First World War has been refracted through often lyrical and elegiac poetry. Even the bitterness of Sassoon in poetry remains contained within perfect rhythmic and poetic forms of expression. Barker's prose is as far removed from, say, Edward Thomas' poem 'Adlestrop' ('Yes, I remember Adlestrop …') as possible. Interestingly, she offers yet another perspective on the conflict – from the viewpoint of a coterie of art students volunteering for the frontline hospitals – in her recent novel *Life Class* (2007).

The critic Fredric Jameson raises a challenging question in this context: he sees such fiction as **pastiche**, stating that the

> ... historical novel can no longer set out to represent the historical past; it can only 'represent' our ideas and stereotypes about the past.

Sebastian Faulks's *Birdsong* (1993) confronts this dual perspective by weaving together an evocation of the First World War with the reactions of his character Elizabeth, in 1978, where Elizabeth mirrors the unknowing modern reader. She is puzzled by the Thiepval Memorial, unable to grasp the meaning of the columns of ascending names:

> 'Who are these, these ...?' She gestured with her hand.
> 'These?' The man with the brush sounded surprised. 'The lost.'
> 'Men who died in this battle?'
> 'No. The lost, the ones they did not find. The others are in the cemeteries.'
> 'These are just the ... unfound?'
> ...
> 'When she could speak again, she said, 'From the whole war?'
> The man shook his head. 'Just these fields.' He gestured with his arm.
> ...
> 'Nobody told me ... My God, nobody told me.'

Looking at the 'annihilating abstractions of Thiepval' from the distance of two generations is also a significant moment in Barker's *Another World*, when Nick visits the battlefields and cemeteries with his grandfather. Like Elizabeth, Nick feels unprepared for the experience; he stares at the memorial and is 'repelled by it'.

The post-war experience

Robert Edric's *Peacetime* (2002) depicts a remote community on the Fenland coast which is seen to be devastated by the changes that have come about as a result of the Second World War. Individuals who have emerged from the war are seen to be blighted by their experience and incapable of returning to their pre-war existences. Mathias, a German prisoner of war, left his family's rose-growing business, seeing war as an escape; yet when he is captured he is occupied with farming in the Pas de Calais to supply German provisions. His family, along with the roses, have all been destroyed in the raids on Hamburg. He has befriended Jacob, a Dutch Jew liberated from the concentration camp at Belsen, who is quite unable to find welcome in the isolated Fenland world. The novel is full of the weight of the violence of the past, a violence that lies beyond articulation:

> 'I saw what they did, you know.'
> 'Sorry? Saw what?'

> 'What they did. Those places. A terrible thing, terrible.'
> 'Oh, I see.'
> 'It's not something you can easily take in.'

This elliptical exchange, between two men who have both fought, is all that can be said of the concentration camps. There is brutality and prejudice here; no 'brave new world' emerges from the rubble, yet there are glimmers of a redemptive decency. Jacob has been cared for by Mathias, who insists that he has done only what

> '... any one man might have done for another.'
> 'Not for a Jew,' Jacob said.
> 'Yes, for a Jew,' Mathias told him firmly.

Amongst the many novels set amongst the drama of active conflict, Edric has chosen to explore a different perspective. His most recent novel, *The Kingdom of Ashes* (2007) is set in post-war Germany, again exploring the moral complexities of the post-war world. His work is subtle and troubling. The Fenland community of *Peacetime* seems stranded in its introspection, a world of fear and hostility in a bleak unyielding landscape. The central protagonist, Mercer, perceives at the end of the novel that they are all indelibly changed by the events of the past years, and that this is a burden they cannot escape:

> Though already a year dead, the war, or so it seemed to Mercer, still clung to everything it had once touched, having lasted too long and been elsewhere too destructive and all-consuming to leave no frayed edges, no ineradicable stains and no blighted men and women fighting in its wake. They had all, he now understood, confused the dying tremors of that violent past with its lasting reverberations into all their futures.

▶ Thinking about the quotation above, and the presentation of a society changed by war, discuss how any one or more texts explores the effects of violent conflict upon the individual. You might also consider why novels such as *Birdsong* move between different generations in their evocation of the First World War.

The novel and the end: millennial anxieties

> Industrial pollution surges, environmental terrors reign, and plagues and earthquakes spread. Our pleasures have become our pains: our food and drink, our sex and smoking, all threaten to injure us. We have new visions of choking, collapsed, crime- and drug-ridden cities, wasted landscapes, fundamentalist conflicts and genocidal wars,

shrinking ice-caps, the widening of the ozone hole.

... Seen from this turning-point, our century is most likely to seem uniquely terrible, less the age of visionary hopes and futuristic utopian prospects ... more a time of terrors, crimes, political disasters and technological horrors.

(Malcolm Bradbury *The Modern British Novel*, 1993)

There is perhaps no genre more suited to the articulation of millennial anxieties than the novel. It is a form that traditionally pursues a linear progress where event produces consequences. Fiction ultimately derives from a view of the universe which assumes that, as human beings, we progress through earthly time until the moment of our individual demise. Beyond personal destiny lies the concept of apocalypse, whether or not religious: time itself will end in a sphere beyond the mortal and transitory. Even in a secular age, this framework of time and narrative still exists. There are few novels that do not conform to a recognised structure whereby some form of narrative **closure** – even if playfully **metafictional** – ends the text. But novels reflect their time. The 9/11 bombings of the World Trade Centre in 2001 and the 7/7 bombings in London in 2005 have introduced a degree of narrative uncertainty and apocalyptic pessimism to the genre. Indeed, the quotation from Bradbury above defines the late 20th-century novel as inherently apocalyptic.

The novel has, of course, always concerned itself with the fates of individuals, lovers, families, societies. Warfare is a popular choice of context because the circumstance heightens emotion: farewells are poignant, sudden and violent death is feared and expected. The irruption of a period of historical chaos into individual lives has produced haunting and memorable fiction. But even the most powerful writing about the two world wars of the 20th century is encountered with a degree of knowledge: the reader is conscious of 'the end'. The individuals whose lives are charted in the text may not survive, narrative suspense can be heightened not obviated, but the broader scheme of events is predictable: in 1918 the Armistice will be signed, in 1945 war in Europe will cease. Within the framework of documented history there can be no narrative surprises – we know what happens in the end. The horror of two world wars is viewed from the distance of one or more generations. The conclusion to *Birdsong* is the joyous birth of Elizabeth's baby, in England in 1979. But with suicide bombing, narrative certainty and futuristic complacency disappear. The moral investigation which may also form part of the novel alters too: in novels about Hitler's 'Final Solution' clear moral codes operate and there is a clearly designed area of individual and collective aberration. History has meaning:

History relates a series of past events in a way that will enable the reader to make sense of them systematically, and to relate them to her own experience. Essential to history is the idea that time has passed and that the past is different from the present. The reader is asked to reason and understand; her pleasure arises from a sense that perspective has been achieved upon events that previously seemed chaotic or meaningless.

(Jane Smiley *Thirteen Ways of Looking at the Novel*, 2006)

Apocalyptic fictions have always existed, often within the genre of science fiction. The telling question now is whether fiction from the post-9/11 perspective is different: we now fear the possibility of the end, what the theorist Baudrillard, in *The Illusion of the End* (1992), has called 'the end of the end'.

J.G. Ballard, a writer who has often chosen to confront extreme circumstances, satirises such cultural anxieties in *Millennium People* (2003). In the chapter a 'Bonfire of the Volvos', Ballard presents an 'upholstered Apocalypse' where London's middle classes briefly rebel, laying waste the exclusive Chelsea Marina before returning to the status quo and moving back in. There is comedy here: the narrator observes that 'when Armageddon takes place, parking is going to be a major problem'. Yet there is also a probing suggestion that the city is inherently alienating. Speaking of a huge estate of 'starter homes' in the shadow of Heathrow, the narrator observes:

> They like that. They like the alienation … There's no past and no future. If they can, they opt for zones without meaning – airports, shopping malls, motorways, car parks. They're in flight from the real.

And it is principally boredom that motivates the protagonist to search for the reason behind the Heathrow bomb which has killed his former wife, his 'quest for Laura's murderer was a search for a more intense and driven experience'.

American writers could be expected to engage with the catastrophic within their world and arguably the bleakest evocation of a post-apocalyptic world is Cormac McCarthy's *The Road* (2006). Here, father and son stagger south through a desolate wasteland, in the belief that reaching the sea might offer some renewal and in the knowledge that they cannot survive a winter in the north. Cities have been incinerated, nature destroyed and the few survivors warily avoid each other, knowing that predatory cannibalistic bands prey on the weak. The dying father offers words of encouragement to his son, as he must, but the reader can only feel that there are too few indications of life to offer any real prospect of hope:

> The days sloughed past uncounted and uncalendared. Along the interstate in the distance long lines of charred and rusting cars. The raw rims of the wheels sitting in a stiff gray sludge of melted rubber, in blackened rings of wire. The incinerated corpses shrunk to the size of a child and propped on the bare springs of the seats. Ten thousand

dreams ensepulchred within their crozzled hearts. They went on. Treading the dead world under like rats on a wheel. The nights dead still and deader black. So cold.

Beneath the unsparing and implacable prose lies the recollection of a world in which father and son go camping, go hunting for food and play games of survival. Occasional glimpses of the familiar heighten the nightmare surrealism of the world that is left. In a ruined supermarket lie a pile of coins and, buried within a pilfered machine, a cold cylinder: a single Coca Cola.

[The boy] looked at his father and then tilted the can and drank. He sat there thinking about it. It's really good, he said.
Yes. It is.
You have some, Papa.
I want you to drink it.
You have some.
He took the can and sipped and handed it back. You drink it, he said. Let's just sit here.
It's because I won't ever get to drink another one, isn't it?
Ever's a long time.
Okay, the boy said.

Don DeLillo's *Falling Man* (2007) and Jay McInerney's *The Good Life* (2006), both concerned with the emotional fall-out from the attacks on New York, offer a radically different moral perspective. McInerney depicts the sumptuous moneyed world of Manhattan's wealthy elite, powerfully evoked as complacent and corrupt. After the destruction of 9/11, certain individuals recoil from the materialism and exploitative sexuality of their previous existences. Yet the Christmas party that concludes the text appears to suggest that, after the initial shock of loss and deliverance, they will all go on, much as before: 'the satori flash of acute wakefulness and connectedness that had followed the initial confrontation with mortality in September was already fading behind them'.

AIDS and the post-1990 novel

A further apocalyptic theme of the post-1990s novel is AIDS, lurking dangerously through Hollinghurst's *The Line of Beauty* or Irving Welsh's *Trainspotting*, and forming the subject of Colm Tóibín's *The Blackwater Lightship* (1999), where the theme gains greater poignancy from the rural and Catholic setting. Tóibín's novel is a quiet domestic drama focusing upon the silence surrounding the subject of AIDS: one young activist defending his gay identity becomes aware when confessing to his mother that she had anticipated his painful revelation was to be membership of the IRA. He remarks sombrely that she would have found that more acceptable.

In *The Line of Beauty*, Hollinghurst chooses to reveal the knee-jerk prejudice that arises once 'this bloody plague' becomes public knowledge: when discussing the death of a well-known actor, a particularly conventional upper-class couple retreat into shocked exclamations and generalisations, 'brought it on [themselves] … they're going to have to learn, aren't they?' Hollinghurst's tone is mocking and satiric: the two young men involved in the discussion are both irresistibly drawn to the world of cocaine and gay sex which is being deplored. In *Trainspotting*, Irvine Welsh creates a far darker and infinitely more destructive effect, as the Edinburgh world he describes is victim to a merciless world of heroin suppliers and used syringes. Perhaps the most radical image comes from Michael Cunningham in *The Hours* (1998). The novel derives its identity from Virginia Woolf's *Mrs Dalloway* (1925) where the distraught and shell-shocked Septimus Smith chooses to commit suicide as a response to the incomprehension of the world he returns to after the war. In Cunningham's work it is Richard, dying of AIDS, who, precisely like Septimus, will leap from the window to his death. European readers might question whether the American victims of AIDS should be equated with the experience of the First World War. Cunningham clearly wants to suggest that AIDS is truly obliterating an entire generation in a horrific and brutal way.

▶ Consider how different writers explore apocalyptic subjects: thinking about the example above from *The Hours*, consider whether different cultural perspectives are important in this context.

Intertextuality and postmodernism

When the novel as a form becomes increasingly self-conscious, it is often described as metafictional. This literally means fiction which is about fiction; the author reminds us that as readers we are engaged with the business of reading a story. The Italian writer Italo Calvino commences *If on a Winter's Night a Traveller* (first translated into English, 1981) with advice to the reader to be comfortable, seek the best chair, close the door, settle down. Michael Cunningham's *The Hours* is an excellent example of the sophisticated techniques of metafiction: as the knowing reader constantly seeks patterns or inevitabilities in the text, the story is not just Cunningham's but also Virginia Woolf's. Post-1990 fiction has seen a number of novels which take as their point of departure a previous literary work. Jane Smiley's *A Thousand Acres*, based on Shakespeare's *King Lear*, is discussed in Part 2 (see page 48). Smiley reinterprets Shakespeare's tragedy to make radical suggestions about the domestic world of a remote rural landscape. Marina Warner, similarly, chooses to reinvent *The Tempest* in her allusive novel *Indigo* (1993). At times, the author may choose this model as a means of exploring moral and political situations: Zadie Smith in *On Beauty* (2006) draws upon E.M. Forster's early

20th-century novel *Howards End* to make contemporary points about sexual politics and race, where Forster was concerned with sex and class.

One notable fictional response to a world perceived as rootless and meaningless can be found in Julian Barnes's *England, England* (1998), a novel in which artifice takes over completely from reality. A powerful entrepreneur decides to create the perfect 'England' as an up-market tourist attraction on the Isle of Wight. A carefully controlled microcosmic world featuring iconic characters and moments of history evolves. England itself is left to crumble into a pre-industrial state, neither dystopian nor idealised. The novel is mocking and ironic: Barnes suggests that contemporary Britain is all too willing to sell itself as a themed heritage site, peddling an invented patriotic nostalgia. Further, he suggests that the artificial product is far more popular than the original. The consumer has no innate sense of 'reality', but happily believes the prettified version on offer. This pessimistic vision, in which there are no satisfactory relationships between individuals, is characteristic of **postmodernism**:

> … a world seen as fragmented and decayed, in which communication between human beings is difficult or impossible, and in which commercial and cheapening forces present an insuperable barrier to human or cultural betterment.
>
> (Jeremy Hawthorn *Studying the Novel*, 2005)

Postmodernism is an expression of the intense cultural anxiety that seems characteristic of the millennium; its underlying fear is that perhaps the ultimate discovery will be that there is no longer any such thing as meaning. In Jonathan Coe's *The Closed Circle* (2004), a novel which satirises the Tony Blair era, a New Labour MP, Paul, is troubled by an unguarded political statement he has made. The youthful media student, Malvina, observes that the meaning is no longer relevant; it is only interpretation which matters. Coe is employing postmodernist language to ridicule a modern political world in which 'spin' is all. Malvina argues that Paul's words could have an entirely different emphasis, given a 'smart use of language':

> 'Irony is very modern,' she assured him. 'Very *now*. You see – you don't have to make it clear exactly what you mean any more. In fact, you don't even have to mean what you say, really. That's the beauty of it.'

Assignments

1 Salman Rushdie has commented that literature is in 'the business of finding new angles at which to enter reality.' Choose two passages from Part 3 and discuss how the author has found new ways of exploring the contemporary world.

2 Many writers have seen the novel as an agent of change: as a group discussion, select two novels and discuss how they challenge established views.

3 Compare two or more texts which incorporate historical or biographical fact into the fiction. What do you see as the advantage or disadvantage of this narrative method?

4 Think about the ways in which a contemporary film (such as *Atonement* or *The English Patient*) has altered a literary text and discuss why changes have been made.

2 | Approaches to the texts

- Who is the narrator?

- Realism or magic realism?

- Different cultures and different voices

- How are novels structured?

- Is 'character' still important?

- What about the reader?

Who is the narrator?

Perhaps the first significant decision of a writer will be the choice of narrator, through whom events will unfold and whose perspective will inevitably inform the reader's experience of the text. It has been observed by more than one critic of contemporary fiction that, increasingly, first-person narratives dominate the fictional scene:

> … the majority of novels published in the early 21st century are likely to be written in the first person. Belief in the appropriateness of the narratorial hierarchy of discourse declined over the last century and many novelists now seem to prefer to render one consciousness or narrator in the first person, which is a way of rendering the world that they might see as antithetical to everyday experience.
>
> (Peter Childs *Contemporary Novelists*, 2005)

The third-person or omniscient narrator establishes from the opening of the text an illusion of complete knowledge, and thereby implies that there can be overall clarity of judgement, an impartial perspective which surveys the entire picture from a god-like altitude. The reader is complicit with this 'narratorial hierarchy', accepting facts as given. A completely different relationship exists with the evident partiality of the first-person voice, given all its individual preconceptions and prejudices. To clarify this crucial difference, compare, for example, the openings of two very familiar 19th-century novels: Jane Austen's *Emma* and Charles Dickens' *Great Expectations*. *Emma* begins 'Emma Woodhouse, handsome, clever, and rich …'. While the reader might acknowledge an undercurrent of irony here, there is no immediate impetus to doubt or contradict this statement, whereas a novel beginning 'Hi! I'm the handsome, clever and rich Emma Woodhouse' would elicit a totally different, undoubtedly sceptical, response from the reader. In Dickens'

Great Expectations the protagonist performs his own introduction: 'My father's family name being Pirrip, and my Christian name Philip, my infant tongue could make of both names nothing longer or more explicit than Pip. So, I called myself Pip, and came to be called Pip.' His childhood perspective is both flawed and vulnerable; at the opening of the novel he is alone in a darkening graveyard with only tombstone engravings to take the place of his parents and brothers. The reader understands this to be artifice at two removes: the voice is neither that of Charles Dickens, nor is it the infant Pip; it is the invented narrator who looks back retrospectively, reconsidering the determining experiences of his early life.

When Peter Childs suggests that belief in 'narratorial hierarchy of discourse' has declined, he refers to the inexorable erosion throughout the 20th century of any kind of philosophical belief in the possibility of a single objective voice presenting an absolute point of view. Ours is a world of questions and uncertainties, and the novel reflects that uncertainty through the use of a single questioning voice.

Childhood and narrative

The child narrator is a device familiar from the Victorian novel onwards: the author can exploit here the dichotomy between a child's incomplete or innocent perception and the more worldly adult comprehension of the reader. In contemporary fiction this disparity has been taken a stage further with narrators who have further limitations imposed upon them.

Mark Haddon: *The Curious Incident of the Dog in the Night-Time*

In Mark Haddon's *The Curious Incident of the Dog in the Night-Time* (2003) the narrator is fifteen-year-old Christopher Boone. Although it is never named in the book, he is afflicted with Asperger's Syndrome, as a result of which he is uncannily brilliant with numbers but incapable of comprehending human emotions. People are literally a 'closed book' to him because he lacks the ability to read faces. His educational psychologist supplies him with line drawings of human expressions, but Christopher's attempts to make progress with these fail because 'faces move very quickly'. The text itself has an unconventional physical appearance: it is visually disorientating because of its *sans serif* font; it resembles children's literature, with frequent drawings and diagrams – patterns which Christopher depends upon to make sense of the potentially chaotic world he inhabits. Further, a final Appendix offers a mathematical problem together with its solution, and there is a unique method of numbering chapters, by prime numbers – because Christopher likes them, indeed regards them as an exemplar of life itself:

> I think prime numbers are like life. They are very logical but you could never work out the rules, even if you spent all your time thinking about them.

Yet the novel requires the reader to comprehend, as its narrator cannot, the complex and uneasy adult world Christopher inhabits: his mother has left the family home with a neighbour, in part because of the difficulty of accommodating her son's mental and emotional needs, and his father conceals the truth of this, together with the weekly letters she sends, choosing instead to tell Christopher that his mother has died. An act of unpremeditated violence – the 'curious incident' – kick-starts a chain of unstoppable events. The novel offers a profound insight into consciousness itself: characters and readers alike acquiesce in the social codes and nuances of communication that contemporary society takes for granted; we recognise anger or irritation when confronted by it. But the narrator himself is an exception. When he describes examples of his own autistic behaviour he does so impartially; when he recounts adult speech he is unaware of what lies beneath the surface, or what is unspoken. The effect of this can be comic or it can be deeply poignant and tragic. In the following extract, Christopher's father finds him reading the hidden letters from his mother; he is a patient man, endlessly accepting of his son's everyday obsessions, because he loves him:

> He said, 'Christopher, what the hell are you doing?'
> And I could tell that he was in the room, but his voice sounded tiny and far away, like people's voices sometimes do when I am groaning and I don't want them to be near me.
> And he said, 'What the fuck are you …? That's my cupboard, Christopher. Those are … Oh shit …Shit, shit, shit, shit, shit.'
> Then he said nothing for a while.
> …
> Then he said, 'I'm sorry, Christopher. I'm so, so, sorry.'
> And then I noticed that I had been sick because I could feel something wet all over me, and I could smell it, like when someone is sick at school.
> Then he said, 'You read the letters.'
> Then I could hear that he was crying because his breath sounded all bubbly and wet, like it does when someone has a cold and they have lots of snot in their nose.
> Then he said, 'I did it for your good, Christopher. Honestly I did. I never meant to lie. I just thought … I just thought it was better if you didn't know … that … that I didn't mean to … I was going to show them to you when you were older.'
> Then he was silent again.
> Then he said, 'It was an accident.'
> Then he was silent again.

John Mullan observes in *How Novels Work* (2006) that Christopher always records swearing without comment or comprehension; his lack of empathy means that he is never aware that adult obscenities correspond with the frustration of overwhelming emotion. He is certainly unaware that it is invariably his own actions or words that provoke this response in the adults around him; he, himself, never resorts to swearing: '[It] is the kind of speech that Christopher would never use, for it is the direct expression of feeling. Yet it also stands for the linguistic incompetence of all those normal adults, inadequate in all their different ways.'

David Mitchell: *Black Swan Green*

David Mitchell's *Black Swan Green* (2006) is also written from the perspective of a teenage boy, growing up in a Worcestershire village through the Falklands War (1982) and the punk rock era of the early Thatcher years. Thirteen-year-old Jason Taylor is infinitely more knowing than Christopher Boone: he has a secure grasp of the ruling ethos of his local comprehensive school and knows the importance of not appearing to challenge the perceived norms. In particular, he knows that his poetry writing must be concealed, '… if they knew Eliot Bolivar who gets poems printed in the Black Swan Green parish magazine was me, they'd gouge me to death behind the tennis courts with blunt woodwork tools and spray the Sex Pistols logo on my gravestone'. For the most part, Jason can negotiate this world just as he endures his elder sister's casual insults, '"*Thing*," Julia mewled, "is being *grotesque* … Mum".' But Jason has his own problems, with stammering, and is constantly involved in verbal and intellectual contortions and evasions to avoid public ignominy. Unlike Christopher in *The Curious Incident*, Jason comprehends the minute fine-tuning of teenage taboo: sitting on the school bus three rows from the front is 'too girly a seat for a third-year boy', further back will cause him problems with the ruling gang. And the driver, known as 'Norman Bates' (deranged killer of Hitchcock's film, *Psycho*) is to be avoided at all costs. At home Jason is experiencing the turmoil of parental discord, ultimately separation, while minutely charting his own physical progress through puberty. At school he is marginalised by the bullies who control his classmates. Reversal comes about partly through his discovery of the socially excluded – the gypsies who travel through the countryside, residing briefly in nearby woodland. By the end of the text Jason has resolved some of his daily difficulties – indeed he has conquered the class bully – but he is leaving his family home, to confront an unknown future. His sister reassures him that the story cannot be over:

> I haven't cried about the divorce once. I'm not going to now. No *bloody* way am I crying! I'll be fourteen in a few days.
> 'It'll be all right,' Julia's gentleness makes it worse, 'in the end, Jace.'
> 'It doesn't *feel* very all right.'
> 'That's because it isn't the end.'

In the first-person narrative as in life, the story is not over: the 'story' as told by a youthful narrator will develop through further experience. Christopher's story ends with him partially reconciled to his father and contemplating a future of mathematics; Jason looks at an unknown future in a new school, his father now united with a girlfriend from years ago.

Jonathan Coe: *The Rotters' Club*

Jonathan Coe's *The Rotters' Club* (2001) concludes similarly, suggesting that there are narrative possibilities that lie beyond the text: following a highly emotional interior monologue on the part of Benjamin – intensely full of life and love – the reader is returned to the frame narrators, Patrick and Sophie, who are the next generation:

> Patrick noticed the sudden shadow of melancholy in her eyes and said:
> – Oh, come on Sophie, don't look at it that way. It was a beautiful story. It was full of nice things: friendships, jokes, good experiences, love. It wasn't all doom and gloom.
> – Yes, I know. It's not that, really. It's just that it was so long ago. They were all so young. And Benjamin and my mother went through so much.
> – But look at her now. She's doing fine. Things could hardly be better for her. And for us.
> – I know. That's all true.
> – And it even has a happy ending.
> – Except that it doesn't feel like the ending to me.
> – But stories never end do they? Not really. All you can do is choose a moment to end on. One out of many. And what a moment you found!

▶ Look back at Christopher's narrative (page 43, above) and compare the first-person voice with Tóibín's description of the child's Christmas in Part 3 (pages 97–98). How effectively is the child's perspective conveyed by the two different writers?

Narrative and dystopia

Dystopian literature creates a fantastical world which is the antithesis of an idealised utopia, it often shares characteristics with science fiction and tends to be futuristic. Margaret Atwood's *The Handmaid's Tale* (1985) is, for example, a feminist dystopia where the 'Handmaids' of Gilead are forced to become official breeders: the world has become polluted by toxic chemicals and radiation, the majority of women are sterile and dispensable. The author is creating a grim fantasy of a future world governed entirely by male cruelty and oppression.

Kazuo Ishiguro: *Never Let Me Go*

In Kazuo Ishiguro's *Never Let Me Go* (2005), the reader slowly becomes aware of a horrifying and entirely unimaginable perspective. Ishiguro delineates a world that appears almost banal in its familiarity: during a trip to Norwich the central characters mingle with the crowds in Woolworth's to look at tapes and cards. Yet they live with an unthinkable destiny: they must all donate vital organs until, ultimately, they 'complete'. They have been cloned for this purpose and educated to understand their unavoidable fate. This dystopic subject matter challenges received views of the first-person narrator in a most interesting way: it is generally argued that readers will empathise more readily with a first-person voice – the 'I' voice sharing intimate knowledge of thought and feeling with the reader in a direct one-to-one relationship. But what kind of empathy can there be with Kathy H? At what point does the reader understand the 'meaning' of her narrative? On a first reading, the significance of the novel's opening statement is not yet apparent:

> My name is Kathy H. I'm thirty-one years old, and I've been a carer now for over eleven years. That sounds long enough, I know, but actually they want me to go on for another eight months, until the end of this year.

The reader later begins to perceive the truth but recoils from it. The fundamental premise of the text is too horrifying to accept willingly. Ishiguro structures the text highly effectively: the reader proceeds with growing unease until Miss Lucy, one of the 'guardians' at their school, decides to enlighten her charges. A group of fifteen-year-olds are innocently discussing their future prospects until Miss Lucy tells them directly that they can have no future, and the veiled suggestions and faintly sinister atmosphere become clarified:

> Miss Lucy was now moving her gaze over the lot of us. 'I know you don't mean any harm. But there's just too much talk like this. I hear it all the time, it's been allowed to go on, and it's not right.' I could see more drops coming off the gutter, and landing on her shoulder, but she didn't seem to notice. 'If no one else will talk to you,' she continued, 'then I will. The problem, as I see it, is that you've been told and not told. You've been told, but none of you really understand, and I dare say, some people are quite happy to leave it that way. But I'm not. If you're going to have decent lives, then you've got to know and know properly. None of you will go to America, none of you will be film stars. And none of you will be working in supermarkets as I heard some of you planning the other day. Your lives are set out for you. You'll become adults, then, before you're old, before you're even middle-aged, you'll start to donate your vital organs. That's what each of you was created to do. You're not like the

actors you watch on your videos, you're not even like me. You were brought into this world for a purpose, and your futures, all of them, have been decided.

Thereafter the reader's entire perception of what is 'normal' shifts: the characters inhabit a world which cannot correspond with everyday reality, yet they listen to music, go shopping, fall in love, even consider themselves as 'lucky'. What type of identification or empathy can be shared with the narrator, or with Ruth and Tommy, characters who are vividly realised? Everything here connects with, or must lead to, death – and a death which might be brutal and messy – yet Kathy can astonish the reader with her ability to find meaning, even delight, in her existence:

> I don't want to give the wrong idea about that period at the Kingsfield. A lot of it was really relaxed, almost idyllic.

Ishiguro's choice of first-person narrator validates the emotional life of these characters and makes the reader confront the unthinkable. Suspense is created because the reader longs for redemption for these characters. Perhaps someone might escape – it seems so simple as they wander freely around Norwich. The realisation that they never will is part of the painful experience of this text. In the 19th-century novel we identify with the rebellious first-person narrator such as Jane Eyre, as she struggles to assert her identity against a hostile world; in Ishiguro's text all the characters accept their bleak and brutal destiny.

▶ Read the extract from *Never Let Me Go* in Part 3 (pages 87–88). Analyse the author's use of Kathy as first-person narrator in the light of the subject of the novel.

Narrative and intertextuality

Intertextuality is discussed more fully in Part 4: Critical approaches. It is a term which signifies the way in which a text is read when it is interfused with echoes or transformations of other texts. Michael Cunningham's *The Hours* (1998), for example, draws throughout on Virginia Woolf's *Mrs Dalloway* (1925), as well as the life and death of Woolf herself. Where Woolf's novel features Septimus Smith, a character who chooses suicide as a response to society's inability to understand his post-war trauma, Cunningham's work is haunted by New York's fear of AIDS. The death of Richard in *The Hours* mirrors that of Septimus Smith. The relationship between the two novels is complex and subtle; it is not a question of the latter work taking inspiration from the former – links, ironies, parallels are suggested throughout. Clearly, though, the reading experience is quite different from encountering a wholly self-sufficient narrative: the reader is always conscious of textual relationships, anticipating, for example, the inevitability of death and mental breakdown.

Jane Smiley: *A Thousand Acres*

Jane Smiley's *A Thousand Acres* (1991) transposes Shakespeare's *King Lear* to a contemporary rural American context and the first-person narrator corresponds to the character Goneril in Shakespeare's play. Here, again, the reader encounters an entirely different form of experimentation with narrative form. The novel could stand alone entirely successfully as a tale of the bitter conflicts between generations of an American family. Or it can be refracted through the reader's knowledge of *Lear*, in which case the reader tends to seek out correspondences and anticipate tragedies. Will the novel conclude with the wholesale slaughter the audience witnesses in the theatre? Smiley shifts the moral sympathy so that events are conveyed through the perspective of the two elder daughters. In Shakespeare's play we mistrust and then despise these characters for their avarice and cruelty; Smiley is suggesting that the pre-history of the text has concealed an evil abuse that simmers beneath the surface and has never been confronted.

One of the most climactic scenes of the play is the point at which Regan and Goneril cast their elderly father out of shelter and onto a barren heath in the midst of a storm, an act of deprivation that causes Lear to lose his mind. In the novel, both daughters urge their father to return to his own home before the storm breaks. Rose, the younger sister, urges him 'Let me take you home' in a 'wheedling' tone, but he refuses to acquiesce and screams at Ginny, the narrator, that she is a 'dried-up whore bitch'.

The balance of sympathy has been shifted here: Rose and Ginny are far from perfect individuals but their father is unpredictable and tyrannical. The novelist has taken *Lear* as a point of departure; her choice of first-person narrator takes the reader directly into a vividly realised world of accumulated hatreds and rivalries which can never be satisfactorily resolved. At the end of the play there is despair and grief, but there is also love and forgiveness; in Smiley's novel there is bitterness and a lack of atonement. Ginny, the narrator, is left with an unsolvable riddle: 'how we judge those who have hurt us when they have shown no remorse or even understanding'. The author herself emphasises that this female narrative lies at the heart of her initial perception of the novel, a combination of a bleak and inimical landscape with internal struggle and, ultimately, solitariness.

> When I conceived *A Thousand Acres*, the ideas about Lear's daughters and about agriculture had been knocking around in my mind for fifteen years or so, but the exact moment they jelled was when I was driving down 135 in Northern Iowa in late March 1988. The landscape was flat and cold, lit by a weak winter sun, and as I stared out of the window, the farm fields seemed enormous and isolated. As soon as I said, 'This is where I could set that Lear book,' the whole thing came into my mind, and the image of that bleak landscape

remained through the writing of the book as a talisman to return to every time composition faltered.

(Thirteen Ways of Looking at the Novel, 2006)

First-person narrators can appear in a number of forms. Novelists find this a particularly appropriate means by which to convey the fragmentary and uncertain sense of truth that characterises the contemporary world. It is a means by which the problematic task of finding meaning can be expressed.

▶ Think about the first-person narratives you have studied: suggest why it is an appropriate choice of perspective and consider how the author has used this narrative device effectively.

The omniscient narrator

While it is true to say that the first-person narrative appears to dominate the contemporary scene, the omniscient narrator is not yet dead. It might, though, be argued that the status of omniscience has shifted somewhat. Novelists have sometimes chosen to exploit this literary device to emphasise distance, even alienation. In Coetzee's *Disgrace* (1999), the central protagonist, David Lurie, is initially a character who seems cold and detached: his personal relationships have floundered, his work as a lecturer is performed mechanically and unenthusiastically, and he fails to grasp that his sexuality is selfishly exploitative. The opening of the novel establishes this unengaged personality and his routine, unemotional attitude to his sexual life; even the precise, dry syntax confirms Lurie's emotional sterility:

> For a man of his age, fifty-two, divorced, he has, to his mind, solved the question of sex rather well. On Thursday afternoons he drives to Green Point. Punctually at two p.m. he presses the buzzer at the entrance to Windsor Mansions, speaks his name, and enters. Waiting for him at the door of No. 113 is Soraya.

Similarly, Colm Tóibín in *The Heather Blazing* (1992) creates a protagonist, Eamon, whose feelings appear numbed and whose adult relationships seem cool. Here, though, this is clearly a reaction to the losses and grief of early childhood. He has developed a protective shell which appears to make him remote from engagement with everyday life, even from those he loves. His world is that of the High Court, where he sits in judgement and can make careful legalistic decisions. When she is dying, his wife accuses him – perhaps for the first time – of learning to sound bored when she speaks of her feelings:

> 'You've always been so distant, so far away from everybody. It is so hard to know you, you let me see so little of you. I watch you

sometimes and wonder if you will ever let any of us know you.'

'I'm trying to help you all day,' he said.

'You don't love me.' She put her arms around him. 'You don't love any of us.'

'Carmel, I do, I do love you.'

'Years ago I tried to tell you about my father and my mother and how much they fought and argued when I was a child, and how much he drank, and no matter what he did how much we preferred him to her, and how handsome I thought he was. Eamon, are you listening to me? Already you are thinking about something else.'

As a child, Eamon has been surrounded by lives full of feeling, indeed burning with Catholic and Nationalist beliefs. The title refers to a Fenian song (see Part 3, pages 97–98) heard with rapt attention on Christmas Day. It is a moment of complete unity: Eamon himself is loved and cherished within this family circle, yet for him the heather will not blaze – passion of any kind seems unattainable. In this context, the omniscient narrator is the most appropriate means of demonstrating the gulf between Eamon and his world.

▶ Using any of the relevant extracts in Part 3 as a starting point, consider how any novelist you have studied uses the omniscient narrative. Suggest why it seems an appropriate choice.

Realism or magic realism?

Realism is so intrinsic to the genre of the novel that the reader tends to accept it unquestioningly. Fiction deals with characters who must, inevitably, inhabit a world – their actions, decisions, emotions are contained within that realised world. When the author creates a recognisable context, full of familiar landmarks, the reader identifies with it in a particular way. It is 'fiction at its familiar work of exploring the world as in general we see it, and the way we live now' (Malcolm Bradbury *The Modern British Novel*, revised 2001). The realist novel can become a form of social document as it was in the 19th century when Dickens sought to alert his readers to uncomfortable truths about their society. The choice of contemporary realism involves the reader in the text: if the modern world is the stuff of fiction, then perhaps life itself is correspondingly exciting. As the author Jane Smiley observes, the 'realistic novel expresses the idea that normal life is intrinsically interesting'. The author might also be suggesting the paradox that the boringly normal – the banal – might itself be remarkable. In E. Annie Proulx's *The Shipping News* (1993), the central character Quoyle has known a poor life of rejections and betrayals, but discovers at the end of the text that the dull routines of life can offer beauty: 'moments in all colors' and that 'love sometimes occurs without pain or misery'.

The geographical present

Graham Swift's *The Light of Day* (2003) emphasises the reality of the city: 'Putney Bridge. The river, black and invisible, below. Putney High Street: the blaze of shops. Superdrug, Body Shop, Marks and Spencer. This safe familiar world.' Swift himself, indeed, discussing the genesis of the text speaks of Wimbledon as 'hardly a more prosaic and unthreatening setting', but within this everyday world he is concerned to trace 'lines of inner geography'. Within this seemingly dull landscape, his few characters inhabit a world of intense passions – desire, betrayal and murderous jealousy.

In Ian McEwan's novels, factual realism is often taken further with the addition of passages of specific medical information which shed light upon central aspects of the text. *Saturday* (2005), in common with a number of contemporary novels, depends upon an entirely accurate geography – the journeys made by the central character Henry Perowne during the course of his day could be followed by any reader with a London A–Z. The political history of the text is also precisely located – it is Saturday 15 February, 2003, the day of the major anti-Iraq war demonstration in London. All the events of the text are known and felt through the character of Perowne. He is a neurosurgeon and two of his operations are described in detail in the novel. McEwan acknowledges, in an afterword to the text, his debt to the consultant neurosurgeon to whom he owes his medical information: 'It was a privilege to watch this gifted surgeon at work in the theatre over a period of two years …'. It is, to say the least, unusual to encounter such a reference as 'for an account of a transsphenoidal hypophysectomy …' in a work of fiction. Why, then does a contemporary writer seek to buttress his work with this degree of technical information? The events of Perowne's day belong securely to the world of fiction: a problematic and violent encounter with a trio of thugs, family meetings with his senile mother and adult children, a dangerous and explosive climax bringing together the various elements of his day. No reader would turn to a novel for an account of brain surgery; however accurately observed and described, technical language belongs to the text book, not the novel.

It is worth comparing McEwan's *Enduring Love* (1997) where knowledge of de Clérambault's syndrome is central to understanding the text. Here, McEwan uses the first-person narrator, Joe, to explain the condition – typically, a homo-erotic obsession with religious overtones. Joe is a rational and undramatic personality, likeable for his attempt to preserve a sane ordinariness in his existence. He is systematically destroyed by the 'psychological terrorism' of a stranger's obsession and the central relationship of his life, his love for Clarissa, is damaged, possibly irrevocably. *Enduring Love* concludes with an Appendix citing the *British Review of Psychiatry*, including more than a page of academic referencing. We have to ask what is achieved by incorporating the apparently factual within the fictional text.

It could be seen as a scientific enforcing of the central thrust of the novel, that within a seemingly normal and unremarkable world the random and destructive can erupt and destroy. At the opening of the text, a totally unpredictable accident involves bystanders; this triggers an emotional response which, for Joe, threatens the end of domestic tranquillity as he becomes the victim of a deranged fantasy.

The historical present

There are a number of possible approaches to using the factual as a narrative device. First, the effect of actuality itself – the densely realised detail of the text confirms to the contemporary reader that this is a wholly familiar world, both at the domestic level and at a more significant political and historical moment. Once the reader is engaged with such familiarity, the anxieties of the text communicate themselves in a very direct way. In *Saturday*, McEwan weaves together most effectively the specific threat of violence – a brutal attack on Perowne, a knife held to the throat of his wife, the possibility that his daughter might be raped – with the insidious threat of unknown terrorism. He opens the novel with Perowne's reflections on the possibility of an aircraft disaster. It is vividly described and is no more than an imaginative flight of fancy, but it is doubtless a waking nightmare that all his readers will comprehend. Perowne's pessimistic reading of the crippled plane passing overhead in the night sky is precipitated by the universal mood following the 9/11 attacks on New York. He has initially resisted subsequent doom-laden prophecies, but gradually his mind has altered to accept the possibility of unknown danger. In a metaphor appropriate to his vocation,

> … he's adapting, the way patients eventually do to their sudden loss of sight or use of their limbs. No going back. The nineties are looking like an innocent decade, and who would have thought that at the time? Now we breathe a different air. He bought Fred Halliday's book and read in the opening pages what looks like a conclusion and a curse: the New York attacks precipitated a global crisis that would, if we were lucky, take a hundred years to resolve. *If we were lucky.* Henry's lifetime, and all of Theo's and Daisy's. And their children's lifetimes too. A Hundred Years' War.

It is apparently possible for the mind to become accustomed to the unthinkable. By the end of the text, the reader comprehends the appropriateness of Perowne's profession: he has studied the aberrations of the human brain and he mends minds. When he is confronted in the street, he is threatened by random and pointless violence – an unjustified attack which could nonetheless leave him seriously injured. Perowne sees in the leader of the group, Baxter, all the signs of a rare mental disease. He makes his diagnosis and causes the diversion which will rescue the situation: 'Your father had it. Now you've got it too.' Like a mass-produced car, an individual brain can be impaired:

> This is how the brilliant machinery of being is undone by the tiniest of faulty cogs, the insidious whisper of ruin, a single bad idea lodged in every cell …

The novel is rooted in accuracy: Perowne's diagnosis of Baxter is correct and the apocalyptic anxieties of the text are validated. There is no rational reason for Baxter to attack Perowne; there may, equally, be no rational reason for fundamentalist terrorists to attack New York and London, but both become possible.

Here, then, McEwan achieves far more than a 'slice of life' realism: the actuality of the text is not background but supplies the dominant metaphor of the novel – damaged minds. And the preciseness of the historical moment endorses the fear within the text.

This combination of fictional events and scrupulous authorial research can also be seen in Jonathan Coe's *The Rotters' Club*, where the contemporary framework leads the reader:

> Backwards in time … Back to a country that neither of us would recognise, probably. Britain, 1973 … a world without mobiles or videos or Playstations or even faxes. A world that had never heard of Princess Diana or Tony Blair, never thought for a moment of going to war in Kosovo or Afghanistan … Imagine!

Coe also juxtaposes the fictional against the historical reality of the Birmingham pub bombings, the industrial conflicts of the British motor industry and the rise of the National Front. He too acknowledges non-fictional sources that have formed a vital part of the discussion within the text, as well as its events.

▶ Think about the quotation from Swift's *The Light of Day* ('This safe familiar world', page 51, above) and discuss the implications of precise description of the contemporary urban world. Suggest why such narrative accuracy might be important to the text.

Hyper-realism

At times an author chooses to emphasise, to a seemingly absurd degree, the realistic minutiae of everyday life: an exaggerated accumulation of detail which might seem to parody realist technique. Tim Pears' *Blenheim Orchard* (2007) is an example of this:

> Ezra Pepin stretched up above the fitted cabinets in the kitchen, clapped cereal packets together, and brought them two at a time to the table. Weetabix and Cheerios. Cornflakes and Shredded Wheat.

Extending his long arms, reaping Oaty Bites and Shreddies, Golden Grahams and Bran Flakes ... Sugar Puffs and Frosties. Special K and All Bran.

The reader might regard this excess as unrealistic: what family serves the entire content of the supermarket at breakfast? But what is its purpose? Ezra Pepin, the middle-aged father described here, has been an anthropologist and studied, in his youth, a remote Paraguayan tribe; during the time of the novel he is a weekend columnist, writing on the foibles of modern life. It is perhaps the author's intention to suggest that the familiarities of everyday existence are as bizarre as any obscure tribe. This is a technique which works effectively in conjunction with either gothic horror or a shocking fact beneath the apparently 'normal' veneer. In Pears' text, there is much simmering beneath the surface of this middle-class Oxford family and finally there is collapse. No amount of reassuring cereal packets has been able to protect them from their own hypocrisies and aberrations. Similarly, a novel such as Roddy Doyle's *The Woman Who Walked into Doors* (1996) is dense with realistic textual detail, but the entire text operates around the central fact that Paula Spencer lives a lie: for eighteen years of married life she has pretended normality while concealing the fact of her husband's abuse. Truth and lies co-exist in a way that emphasises the unnatural life she leads: the detail is recognisable but the central fact is horrifying and raises a problematic question – why does Paula choose to lie and to remain with a brutally violent husband? In this respect the 'realist' novel can offer complexity rather than simple familiarity. What exactly is 'normal' to Paula as she struggles to survive? Equally, the fabric of Christopher's world in *The Curious Incident of the Dog in the Night-Time* seems unremarkable, but it is conveyed to the reader through a perspective which is entirely unique.

Historical realism

There is a great deal of excellent historical writing in the post-1990 novel. Adam Thorpe, Barry Unsworth and Matthew Kneale, in particular, have all written notable historical fictions, often bringing unfamiliar worlds to light. Part 1 has some discussion of the prevalence of fictional writing in this period, taking as subject the two world wars (pages 30–33), in particular Pat Barker's evocation of the First World War through historical characters such as Siegfried Sassoon and Wilfred Owen. Here, clearly, there needs to be a degree of historical **verisimilitude**, although individual characters and events can be invented. Indeed, the question of realism in war literature is perhaps challenging. Readers tend to be familiar with events described and it could be argued that film has saturated the contemporary imagination with powerful images of both conflicts.

Michael Ondaatje: *The English Patient*

Ondaatje's *The English Patient* (1992) is set in the Second World War and is a complex collage of different narrators and time-scales; it is rich in literature, legend and fantasy as well as carefully researched historical fact. The eponymous protagonist, Almásy, is based on a 'real' person, a Hungarian aviator and desert explorer of the period, yet in the novel he seems apart from historical realism: his obsessions are the timelessness of the desert and his passionate love for Katharine Clifton. The war will intrude upon his life, completely changing it, yet he is wholly uninterested in the course of the war – he identifies with England and its traditions, but offers help to Rommel, Hitler's General in Africa, and acts as a guide to German spies who wish to avoid Allied forces in the desert and to enter Cairo. He carries everywhere with him his copy of the histories of the ancient Greek writer Herodotus, and it is perhaps this reading which gives him a sense that individual lives are insignificant in the vastness and emptiness of the desert.

> So a man in the desert can slip into a name as if within a discovered well, and in its shadowed coolness be tempted never to leave such containment. My great desire was to remain there, among those acacias. I was walking not in a place where no one had walked before but in a place where there were sudden brief populations over the centuries … and in between these times – nothing was there … Sporadic appearances and disappearances, like legends and rumours through history.

In 1936 Almásy is travelling with members of the Geographical Society, charting areas of desert and searching for a lost and ancient oasis. He meets the newly married Katharine Clifton and they fall in love. The tragedy of the love affair is that its dramatic climax occurs in the last few days before war breaks out. Katharine's jealous husband attempts to crash in the desert in such a way that all three will be killed. Almásy rescues the injured Katharine from the burning plane, but it will be three years before he can return to the Cave of Swimmers where he has sought refuge for her. Captured by British troops, he can only get back when he volunteers his knowledge of the desert to Rommel – 'a brilliant man'. The focus in this novel is on an intensely private individual, devoid of any loyalty to either British or German interests; indeed, he is not the 'English patient' at all, but the Hungarian Count Lázló de Almásy. He is unmasked by Caravaggio, a Canadian who has been tortured by the retreating Germans and who is determined to discover the truth of Almásy's tale and the depths of his betrayals. Despite his own suffering, and permanent disfigurement, Caravaggio can conclude of Almásy, 'It no longer matters which side he was on during the war.' Yet Ondaatje is careful to emphasise the realism of aspects of his writing: he acknowledges sources and archives and cites an army text, *Unexploded Bomb*, from which he quotes in the sections dealing with the

Sikh sapper Kurpal Singh (Kip). The author makes use of a tradition of realism in the text as if to validate the novel, but he suggests that the catastrophic movements of war – armies burning their way across the Sahara, broken individuals torn and bleeding from savage acts of reprisal – are transient moments of history, and that for one man the English and the Germans are just means to try to recover the body of the woman he has loved. The war is simply in his way.

Novel into film

Antony Minghella's film of the novel (1996) supplies an interesting footnote: he chose to emphasise the love story of the tale, ignoring Ondaatje's conclusion of the novel – with Kip's horror at the dropping of the atom bomb on Hiroshima, and his eventual return to India. The film was favourably received. American reviewers preferred it to the novel, rejecting the novel's ending as 'crude polemic'. It has been argued that the novel offers a **critique** of the 20th century's most powerful cultural myth, 'the narrative of western sacrifice, heroism and ultimate sacrifice in the "Good War"'; Minghella prefers to focus on the romance of Almásy's story, rather than convey Ondaatje's anti-European perspective.

▶ What is your own judgement of the relationship between Minghella's film and Ondaatje's novel? Do you agree that there is a degree of falsification, or simplification, of Ondaatje's written text?

In other contexts, the war might be seen as an opportunity. Sarah Waters' *The Night Watch* (2006) portrays characters inhabiting a London which is being devastated by the Blitz. Life and love is heightened by the possibility of imminent death; more particularly the (forbidden) lesbian affairs of the text can flourish. The end of the war reintroduces a degree of inhibition:

> 'Don't you know the war's over?' the man behind the counter in a baker's shop asked Kay.
>
> He said it because of her trousers and hair, trying to be funny; but she had heard this sort of thing a thousand times, and it was hard to smile. When he caught her accent, anyway, his manner changed. He handed over the bag, saying, 'There you are, madam.' But he must have given some sort of look behind her back because as she went out, the other customers laughed.
>
> She was used to that too.

Magic realism

Magic realism is a term denoting the conjunction of the realistic and 'normal' with the extraordinary and wholly impossible. The best examples of this in contemporary writing can be found in the works of the Czech writer Milan Kundera and, in English, Salman Rushdie. At the opening of the latter's *The Satanic Verses,* the two principal characters fall from an exploded plane, singing, and land unharmed on a snow-covered English beach. David Lodge, novelist and critic, suggests that there is a reason for this late 20th-century combining of realism with its apparent opposite:

> [These] writers have lived through great historical convulsions and wrenching personal upheavals, which they feel cannot be adequately represented in a discourse of undisturbed realism.
>
> (*The Art of Fiction*, 1992)

Magic realism can be witty and playful, mocking the reader's expectations with a dazzling display of impossibilities. This is fiction that challenges the reader's willing suspension of disbelief: a realistically embodied world is created, but within that world the most extreme and improbable events occur.

Angela Carter: *Wise Children*

An excellent example of this is Angela Carter's *Wise Children* (1991), an exuberant updated version of Shakespearean comedy, complete with all the improbabilities of multiple pairs of twins, confused identities, unexpected sexual liaisons and consequent parenting, all set in a theatrical world of disguise, grease paint and alcoholic partying. The narrator is Dora Chance, one of the illegitimate twins of legendary Shakespearean tragedian, Sir Melchior Hazard; hers is an incorrigibly lively voice recalling a lifetime of music hall song and dance. As the child from the 'wrong side of the tracks', her voice will never carry the serious weight of Shakespearean tragedy. The novel commences with an invitation to her father's 100th birthday party and concludes with the outrageous revelations and appearances which burst upon the party itself – rather like the revelations which occur at the end of one of Shakespeare's comedies. At the climax of the event a huge birthday cake in the shape of the Globe Theatre is produced, with a theatrical sword for the centenarian actor to cut:

> What happened was this: drumroll, flames, hush, uplifted cake knife but, before it could descend, came a tremendous knocking at the front door. TREMENDOUS. Such a knocking that the birthday candles dipped and swayed and dropped wax on the chocolate tiles; the boughs of lilac tossed, scattering nodes of bloom; the very parquet underneath us seemed to tremble, about to rise up.
>
> A thrill ran through the room. Something unscripted is about to happen.

And in bursts Melchior's twin brother Peregrine, long believed dead, and with him dozens of colourful butterflies – a perfectly managed stage entrance. Peregrine's role is to reveal that the legitimate daughters of the respectable Sir Melchior have, in fact, been fathered by himself. Following this revelation, despite his advanced years, he proceeds upstairs for an energetic, chandelier-shaking bout of sexual gymnastics with his niece, Dora. The novel both mocks and delights in the extravagances of stage comedy, the theatrical context suggesting that Nora's and Dora's life on the 'wrong side of the tracks' is infinitely more exciting than the duller life of their supposedly-legitimate half-sisters. (See also the extract from *Wise Children* in Part 3, pages 84–85.)

Yann Martel: *Life of Pi*

There are many contemporary texts that seek to challenge conventional depictions of realism: Yann Martel's *Life of Pi* (2001) is a curious tale which, to the *Financial Times* reviewer, suggested 'Joseph Conrad and Salman Rushdie hallucinating together over the meaning of *The Old Man and the Sea* and *Gulliver's Travels*'. The majority of the text is an account of the survival of the protagonist Piscine Patel, or Pi, castaway from a sinking ship with only the company of a Bengal tiger, improbably named Richard Parker. The text has all the minutiae of detail which characterises *Robinson Crusoe*: the determined struggle to survive, the practicalities of ingenious methods of securing food and water, the psychological sufferings of the solitary mind deprived of human contact. The writer's method, therefore, shares much in common with the realist text – yet the central premise of the novel is unthinkably bizarre. Man and tiger do not, in the 'real world' share food, space, companionship. And the text does not sentimentalise or anthropomorphise Richard Parker in the manner of children's stories: he is a magnificent beast who will naturally kill indiscriminately, indeed must do so to live. The careful attention to realist detail, in particular the insistence upon the physical description of the body, is the means by which Martel commands the reader's attention and maintains conviction. An extract from Pi's account of his average day – if there be such – illustrates this attention to factuality:

> Sunrise to mid-morning:
>> wake up
>> prayers
>> breakfast for Richard Parker
>> general inspection of raft and lifeboat, with particular attention
>> paid to all knots and ropes
>> tending of solar stills (wiping, inflating, topping off with water)
>> breakfast and inspection of food stores
>> fishing and preparing of fish if any caught (gutting, cleaning,
>> hanging of strips of flesh on lines to cure in the sun)

Like Angela Carter, the author writes with a sophisticated perception of the possibilities of the novel and can exploit these in a way that celebrates the possibilities of genre, as well as affirming the value of life itself. Pi's tale is presented through a frame that insists upon the truth of the tale, 'a story that will make you believe in God'. It concludes with a blood-curdling, cannibalistic alternative account to satisfy the disbelief of the Japanese Maritime Department – but they find the substituted version less acceptable.

Jim Crace: *Quarantine*

Jim Crace is a writer who, in a number of novels, is interested in exploring the limits of the genre: *Being Dead* (1999) is an exploration of precisely that state, and in *Quarantine* (1997) a small band of pilgrims embark upon a period of separation and denial in the Judean desert in order to seek purification and renewal. They meet a base and violent merchant, Musa, who attempts to exploit them. They are also aware of the presence of a remote Galilean, Jesus, who pursues his fasting to the ultimate degree, dies in his cave and is buried beneath stones by the other travellers. Crace has said that his interest in the subject is not a religious one: he included the Galilean Jesus primarily as a way of indicating first-century Judaism as his chosen setting for the novel. All the characters depicted have, in their different ways, reached the limits of their endurance of life, which is why they have sought the life apart. They return, not quite able to account for their experiences. Musa has been abandoned by his wife, who grasps the opportunity to escape his brutality, but the merchant, undaunted, manages to find his way back into the city, telling fantastic tales of his experiences. As he looks back at the fringes of desert landscape he sees the unmistakable figure of the Galilean, slowly and with bleeding feet, walking through the shimmering heat.

▶ Thinking about the extract from *Life of Pi*, above, discuss the author's ability to interest readers in the improbable.

End of empire and post-colonial writing

Let me ask you to imagine this. Living far from you is a beloved relation whom you have never met. Yet this relation is so dear a kin she is known as Mother. Your own mummy talks of Mother all the time. 'Oh Mother is a beautiful woman – refined, mannerly and cultured.' Your daddy tells you, 'Mother thinks of you as her children; like the Lord above she takes care of you from afar.' There are many valorous stories told of her, which enthral grown men as well as children. Her photographs are cherished, pinned in your own family album to be admired over and over. Your finest, your best, everything

you have that is worthy is sent to Mother as gifts. And on her
birthday you sing-song and party.

(Andrea Levy *Small Island*)

Fuckin failures in a country ay failures. It's nae good blamin it oan
the English fir colonising us. Ah don't hate the English. They're just
wankers. We are colonised by wankers. We can't even pick a decent,
vibrant, healthy culture to be colonised by. No. We're ruled by effete
arseholes. What does that make us? The lowest of the fuckin low, the
scum of the earth. The most wretched, servile, miserable, pathetic
trash that was ever shat intae creation.

(Irvine Welsh *Trainspotting*)

At the close of the 20th century, end of empire becomes a powerful theme in
fiction. As the two quotations above illustrate, this is far from being a simple issue.
After the Second World War, the British Empire was steadily dismantled: India
and Pakistan gained independence in 1947; the African nations of Kenya, Nigeria,
South Africa and Uganda followed in the 1960s, together with formerly British
Caribbean countries (Jamaica, Barbados, the Bahamas, Dominica). The Irish Free
State was internationally recognised in 1922 and, more recently, Scotland and
Wales have welcomed devolved government. It is not altogether surprising that this
has resulted in a 'literature of farewell', as discussed by Ian Jack (see Part 3, page
83). Late 20th-century fiction is full of a world order which has irretrievably gone.
But there is more than just the 'literature of exhaustion' here: new life and energy is
born from the hybrid complexity of post-colonial writing. English-language novels
naturally include writing by authors whose culture has always been perceived as
British – Scotland, Wales and Northern Ireland in terms of geographical proximity,
but also Australia, New Zealand and Canada. Britain's former colonies have
produced the different perspectives of Africa, India and the West Indies. But the end
of the century and beginning of the next has also witnessed a rich abundance of
fictional writing by writers from formerly colonised nations who have migrated to
Britain. This is not a simple relationship, as critic Elleke Boehmer writes:

Rather than simply being the writing which 'comes after' empire,
post-colonial literature is generally defined as that which critically or
subversively scrutinises the colonial relationship.

(*Colonial and Post-colonial Writing*, 1995)

Writing such as Zadie Smith's *White Teeth* or Monica Ali's *Brick Lane* experiments
with different voices and perspectives in order to convey the complexity of this
new cultural direction. *White Teeth*, in particular, is a novel of extraordinary vitality
and originality. Started before the author had left university, it portrays a youthful
world sophisticated in the complexities of moving daily between different social

and cultural contexts, indeed alert to the many comic ironies of this multiplicity. A prime target of Smith's writing is the liberal, middle-class world of the Chalfen family and the attempts of the London Borough of Brent to adopt multicultural educational policies. *Brick Lane*, written after 9/11, suggests a more searching critique. Chanu despairs over the history that his daughters are taught:

> 'Dark Ages,' said Chanu, and his face flinched from the insult. 'This is what they are calling it in these damn Christian books. Is that what they teach you in school?' He threw the book on the floor. 'It was the Golden Age of Islam, the height of civilisation. Don't forget it. Take pride, or all is lost.' He lay down again, exhausted by the insult.

Meanwhile, British National Party leaflets are constantly delivered to Chanu's door, bemoaning the 'multicultural murder' of English education:

> *'Do you know what they are teaching your children today? In domestic science your daughter will learn how to make a kebab, or fry a bhaji. For his history your son will be studying Africa or India or some other dark and distant land.'*

The novel charts these unresolved difficulties, questioning how far the first-generation experience of immigration is one marked by failure and defeat. It is the concept of individual identity that lies at the heart of this discourse of birth and nationhood. In *White Teeth*, Samad is horrified when his clever nine-year-old son elects to be known as 'Mark Smith' by his chess-club friends:

> 'I GIVE YOU A GLORIOUS NAME LIKE MAGID MAHFOOZ MURSHED MUBTASIM IQBAL! … AND YOU WANT TO BE CALLED MARK SMITH!'

The Irish novel

The question of identity – the search for or attempt to crystallise identity – is often at the forefront of Irish writing. Two novelists considered here have notably complex roots of their own: William Trevor is a Protestant, Anglo-Irish writer from County Cork; Brian Moore is a Catholic writer from Dublin (he later emigrated to America).

The post-1990 period has been a particularly rich one for Irish writing, both in the Republic and the North. On both sides of the border, fiction is seen to grapple with some of the outstanding controversies of the day as well as to reassess events of the past. Fiction, here, is a way of making history personal, of creating vivid drama from the weight of history. Novels such as Roddy Doyle's *The Woman Who Walked into Doors* (1996) and Patrick McCabe's *The Butcher Boy* (1992) are both intensely violent novels, depicting respectively the prolonged abuse of Paula Spencer by her husband, and the sexual abuse of a child by a priest and the child's macabre acts of vengeance. Domestic violence and paedophilia are taboo subjects, undermining any notion of the good Catholic family and suggesting that a conspiracy of silence surrounds and thereby condones such abuse. Here, fiction is bringing to light contemporary truths that have been denied or marginalised, making the challenging suggestion that society is guilty of hypocrisy in leaving such issues undebated and hence denied. In the Irish context, both Doyle and McCabe suggest that post-colonialism is itself a simplified notion: the idea that removing English rule and English Protestantism from Irish soil would result in a new Celtic, Catholic perfection is challenged and found wanting. Roddy Doyle uses a parody of fairy tale language to emphasise the dichotomy between the narrative Paula would like to believe and the uncomfortable truth of her situation; in reality she has moved from a violent and unpredictable father to an abusive husband, 'Once upon a time my life had been good. My parents had loved me. The house was full of laughter. I'd run to school every morning.' In the Irish Republic, fiction has been seen as dangerous: in the 1960s the early novels of Edna O'Brien and John McGahern were banned from sale and publication because their depiction of Irish life was regarded as offensive.

William Trevor: *The Story of Lucy Gault*

Ireland's troubled past is a major subject for fiction, in a tradition from Elizabeth Bowen (1899–1973) to William Trevor. The latter's *The Story of Lucy Gault* treats a traditional theme: the 'Big House', English-owned and as such a symbol of imperial domination over a country seeking independence. In the summer of 1921, the Gaults of Lahardane have been in possession of house and land for two hundred years; the last remaining survivor of the family, Captain Everard Gault, has a profound love of the landscape and the Georgian house he has inherited. He himself has been wounded in the First World War, he has no son to inherit his property, he lives modestly and is a peaceable member of the small rural community. But it is the period of firing the historic Anglo-Irish houses and driving away the English landowners. The novel commences with the poisoning of the Gault's dogs, the discovery of concealed petrol cans and a single shot, fired by Captain Gault to frighten away a trio of youthful arsonists. A letter of sympathy is passed to the parish priest to communicate regret to the family of the injured boy, but the mood of the day is one of opposition to the colonial past, and a subsequent visit to the boy's family to seek reconciliation is unsuccessful. Gault realises that he and his small family can no longer stay. The author presents these opening events in a stark manner, 'Captain Everard Gault wounded the boy in the right shoulder on the night of June the twenty-first, nineteen twenty-one'. The weight of history itself means that the date together with the English name and rank create a degree of inevitability. The 'story' of the title can only be a tragic tale. The focus of Trevor's interest is the unhappy outcome for the child, Lucy. At eight years old she knows nothing of the wider political world she inhabits; she knows only that she clings to the place she loves with even greater longing than her feeling for her parents, even though she is a cherished only child. 'Couldn't I stay with Henry and Bridget?' she constantly asks. She is destined to remain always at Lahardane, after her childish impulse to escape has disastrous consequences. Thereafter her life will become an image of frozen immobility: her parents leave without her, believing that she is drowned. They do not know that she lives and they never return. Love tantalisingly appears in the form of Ralph, but he must marry a sensible young lady, not the strange girl who has become a local myth. And, finally, when her bereaved father comes home, she can only murmur brokenly, 'Why now?' to him.

Lucy is not the only haunted character of the tale: the wounded young man of the opening, Horahan, sinks into a disturbed state, convinced that he has succeeded in burning the house and its inhabitants. Atonement might never come to this tortured individual, but when he sees Captain Gault return to Enniseala as an old man, he feels that the Virgin Mary has spoken to him. He comes to Lahardane and speaks of his actions, a voice that, having spoken, will never utter again. Lucy desires to reproach this man, to articulate the pain of years, 'that she might have married the man she loved, that her father and mother had been driven from their house, that her mother had never recovered from her distress'. She wants to record the destruction, fear and chaos of their lives, but her anger collapses as her father says to this desperate individual, 'Go safely now' – and she simply cries out for all that has been lost to her, 'her anguish echoing in the trees of the avenue, her tears damp on her father's clothes'.

The moral sympathies within the tale are subtle and complex; there is no discussion of the political and historical situation, simply the fact of pre-independence Ireland in the early 1920s. The tragedy of the small cast of characters is finely balanced: the young man Horahan who never escapes visions of burning and Lucy herself who loses irrecoverably both love and future, 'Calamity shaped a life when, long ago, chance was so cruel'. It is an elegiac text, there is no discussion of right or wrong, just the presentation of a remote corner of Ireland at a time of strife.

Colm Tóibín: *The Heather Blazing*

The motif of burning English houses is part of the history and tale-telling of Tóibín's *The Heather Blazing* (1993). Eamon thinks back to the electioneering of his youth: he has campaigned for de Valera and Irish independence and recalls his own impassioned speeches, 'we know how much this country has suffered under foreign rule …'. He discovers that his father as a young man in the 1920s would travel to Dublin on the pretence of studying in the National Library, while, in fact, seeking permission for the burning of local houses:

> 'You couldn't just burn a house, you see,' Uncle Tom said. 'You'd have to get permission from Cathal Brugha in Dublin. You'd have to present him with all the facts; any of the houses that entertained the Black and Tans, had the officers up for dinners and parties, they'd be on the list. Your father'd go up, he was young enough and he pretended to spend the day in the National Library, but he'd slip out to see Brugha, or one of Brugha's men, and then permission would come back and then we'd do the job.'
> 'Burn the house?' Eamon asked.
> 'We gutted a good few of them all right …'
> 'Were they all Protestants?' Eamon asked.
> 'They were … [They] were all up to their necks in the British Army who were on the rampage here, and the British Legion and the King and the Queen. It's all gone now. At least we got rid of that, whatever else we did.'

Eamon recalls this conversation with his father and uncle years later, in the present-day world of the tale, when he is interviewed by a historian who is researching the Irish government's response to the IRA campaign of the early 1970s. The author is thereby making connections across the 20th century, interweaving explosive times and climactic events in Irish history. Eamon himself, full of ideological conviction in his youth, has used his judicial position to warn his government against allowing republican feeling to become inflamed in the south. Looking at this through the eyes of the historian, he is aware that his report could seem cold and calculating, implying that the north should be seen almost as a foreign country, a 'place apart'. He chooses to repress some of this information and reveals little in their civilised exchanges over brandy. Both men have families who have been involved in the epochal events of 1916 but, again, Eamon prefers not to share his own family history. He comments about his father, 'If you asked him, he would grow silent. It was a very bitter time for them.' Thinking about the time in his grandmother's house, he feels increasingly convinced that he should consign his father's story 'to the past, to silence'.

In both novels, the conflicts of the past cannot be eradicated. The struggle to break free from English rule has been a bitter one; it has destroyed individuals and left a legacy of sorrow and silence. Equally, there is no caricature villain in these late 20th-century texts: it would be difficult to characterise Captain Gault as a domineering imperialist presence or Horahan as a crazed zealot.

Brian Moore: *Lies of Silence*

It is worth comparing a novel set in the context of Northern Ireland at the height of the 'Troubles'. In Brian Moore's *Lies of Silence* (1990), Michael Dillon is caught in a dilemma not of his making. As hotel manager to a major Belfast hotel, he is forced by the IRA to drive to work and park his car in his accustomed space (because he alone is not scrutinised by security), knowing that it carries a bomb timed to explode soon after his arrival. If he refuses, his wife will be killed. He chooses to report the bomb to the police, averting disaster, but implicitly proclaiming that his wife's life is a lesser concern to him. By doing this he saves innocent civilians and a major Protestant unionist speaker he detests. Dillon himself is a Catholic, but discovers that there can be no neutrality in the war-zone that is now Belfast. A former school-fellow, now a priest, comes to ask that he should not identify the young assailant who has attacked him and his wife. He refuses to co-operate – his desire is simply to live his own private life and make his own moral judgements, independent of both extremes around him. But this is seen to be impossible and the outcome is disastrous.

▶ Thinking about any one of the novels discussed here, examine the author's treatment of the historical past. How does it influence, or destroy, individual lives?

▶ Discuss whether post-colonialism is a helpful concept in studying Irish writing.

Coetzee and South Africa

Coetzee's *Disgrace* (1999) is set, like Tóibín's novel, at a time after conflict, but which still bears the scars of the colonial past. In the post-apartheid world of the text, there is violence and hatred; *Disgrace* has been seen in South Africa as a controversial novel confronting unpalatable truths and offering no satisfactory resolution. The title itself is troubling and rapidly suggests both sexual and racial implications. Initially, the 'disgrace' is the protagonist's – David Lurie has pursued his sexual desires with little thought beyond his own immediate gratification: he is exploitative and uninvolved. At the beginning of the novel he purchases the favours of 'Soraya', described by her agency as 'Exotic'; she is clearly mixed-race and young enough to be his daughter. He is untroubled by his commodification of sex, and not inclined to engage in any soul-searching when he replaces Soraya with one of his students, Melanie. But an insistent theme within the novel is the notion that times have changed, that a lazy assumption of white middle-class male supremacy is no longer appropriate. His ex-wife rebukes him for his sexual predatoriness:

> Don't expect sympathy from me, David, and don't expect sympathy from anyone else either. No sympathy, no mercy, not in this day and age. Everyone's hand will be against you, and why not?

Disgraced by the university authorities, he seeks refuge with his daughter, Lucy, in the country. But as father and daughter are debating Lurie's situation, indeed, whether desire is no more than 'a burden we could well do without', they are attacked by three African men who shoot Lucy's dogs, beat her father and attempt to set him alight, and repeatedly rape Lucy herself. Now it is Lucy who feels disgraced: she refuses to report the crime and will not undergo an abortion. She lives with the horror that she has experienced an attack of profound personal hatred, that she is the victim of an act of revenge and, as such, an object of 'subjection, subjugation'. She fears that her attackers will return, yet she will not leave. Brooding over the implications of this new South Africa, she questions:

> What if ... what if that is the price one has to pay for staying on? Perhaps *that* is how they look at it; perhaps that is how I should look at it too. They see me as owing something. They see themselves as debt collectors, tax collectors. Why should I be allowed to live here without paying?

Lucy eventually makes over her land to her African co-farmer, Petrus, in return for protection for herself and her child. She is aware that her choice is ignominious but, unlike her father, who has no understanding of her perspective, she can accept that:

> '... I agree, it is humiliating. But perhaps that is a good point to start from again. Perhaps that is what I must learn to accept. To start at ground level. With nothing. Not with nothing but. With nothing. No cards, no weapons, no property, no rights, no dignity.'
> 'Like a dog.'
> 'Yes, like a dog.'

Disgrace is a disturbing book in its treatment of the pain of private shame and its wider social context. There is no post-apartheid utopian vision here, but a menacing awareness that the injustices of history will be avenged. It is also a book which has gained notoriety in South Africa: it was denounced by the ANC, the ruling party, as a racist text, guilty of depicting Lucy's attackers as 'savage, violent and incapable of refinement through education'. The novel was effectively put on trial and referred to the South African Human Rights Commission. Ironically, when Coetzee was awarded the Nobel Prize for Literature in 2003, he was addressed in these terms:

> You are a Truth and Reconciliation Commission on your own ... Unsettling and surprising, you have dug deep into the ground of the human condition with its cruelty and loneliness ... [You] have unveiled the masks of our civilities and uncovered the topography of evil.

Hilary Mantel: *A Change of Climate*

It is revealing to compare *Disgrace* with Hilary Mantel's *A Change of Climate* (1994), which, similarly, treats the painful realities of life in a colonial society, Botswana, formerly known as Bechuanaland. Ralph and Anna Eldred live there as missionaries in violent, apartheid times: they are imprisoned for failing to observe discriminations that white people are meant to take for granted. Later, they are the victims of a horrifying attack on their twin babies. Like Coetzee, Mantel explores the question of how far characters can return to any concept of normality once they have experienced trauma. The novelist Anita Brookner, reviewing *A Change of Climate*, suggested that Mantel, unusually, addresses 'unresolved moral questions'. In both novels, there is no easy solution, no meeting of minds: when David Lurie understands that Lucy will continue with her pregnancy and bring up the child, he feels that 'everything is changed, utterly changed' and for the first time in the novel, breaks down completely:

> Standing in the wall outside the kitchen, hiding his face in his hands, he heaves and heaves and finally cries.

In *A Change of Climate* Ralph and Anna, still young, return to England, have children, live a 'good' life – yet they avoid and suppress the tragedy of the past in a way that can only be destructive. Anna cannot forgive, and abandons her Christian faith; Ralph flings himself into charitable work. Finally the false appearance of control deserts them, just as a character more broken than any they have yet encountered enters their world. At the end of the text, the reader is left questioning whether Anna can embrace 'what is lowest and most unlovable' and rediscover a world of feeling. At the end of *Disgrace,* David Lurie the former university professor, assists with the euthanasia of unwanted dogs.

▶ Looking at the violence of the colonial and post-colonial experience depicted in these novels, consider how far individuals can escape past trauma and envisage a future. Do Coetzee and Mantel offer the reader any optimism?

The post-colonial novel in Britain

Britain's changing identity is, not surprisingly, the subject of a burgeoning number of post-colonial novels, often written from the perspective of the immigrant making the shocked discovery that the reality of English life is very different from expectation.

Andrea Levy: *Small Island*

Andrea Levy's *Small Island* takes the experience of Gilbert Joseph, a Jamaican who has volunteered to fight with the RAF in the Second World War, and who then chooses to come to England in 1948. His new wife, Hortense, will follow shortly after, full of highly elevated expectations of her new life in the 'Mother Country'. But she finds a London almost devastated by the experiences of the war, in particular the Blitz, and full of suspicion and hostility towards her. She is well-educated but mocked; her husband dreams of becoming a lawyer, but settles for driving a Post Office van. Everywhere they encounter a racism they are – at first – quite unprepared for:

> So, how many gates I swing open? How many houses I knock on? Let me count the doors that opened slow and shut quick without even me breath managing to get inside. Man, these English landlords and ladies could come up with excuses. If I had been in uniform – still a Brylcreem boy in blue – would they have seen me different? Would they have thanked me for the sweet victory. Shaken my hand and invited me in for tea? Or would I still see that look of quiet horror pass across their smiling face like a cloud before the sun ...?

The novel is rooted in the experiences of the time, with flashbacks that take the reader to earlier significant events. The contemporary reader is conscious that sixty years have passed since these events; the novel could be considered in the light of historical fiction, as well as a lively account of the struggle of individual lives and loves.

Zadie Smith: *White Teeth*

Zadie Smith's *White Teeth* is an evocation of Willesden, north London, in the 1980s. The language and attitudes of society have changed: although the elderly might still use the unthinking language of previous times, they concede that it is no longer acceptable. Magid and Millat, twin sons of Samad Iqbal, attempt to assure an elderly man, to whom they are delivering harvest fruits, that their father has fought and been injured in the war:

> 'My dad was in the war ... He played for England ...' piped up Millat, red-faced and furious.
> 'Well, boy, do you mean the football team or the army?'
> 'The British Army. He drove a tank. A Mr Churchill ...'
> 'I'm afraid you must be mistaken,' said Mr Hamilton, genteel as ever. 'There were certainly no wogs as I remember – though you're probably not allowed to say that these days are you?'

Samad sees his family's life in London as a series of continual betrayals and disillusionments; his sons reject their Islamic background for the dominant culture that surrounds them. Equally, their friend Irie, the daughter of an English father and Jamaican mother, longs for straight hair rather than her own Afro curls.

However, the novel revels in constantly unfolding ironies: the rebellious teenager, Millat, chooses to identify with the Islamic protest against Salman Rushdie's *Satanic Verses*. Neither he, nor his immediate gang, has read the book, but they identify with the anger articulated. Meanwhile, his brother, who has been sent home to Bangladesh to receive a correct Muslim education, emerges as a perfect English gentleman, entirely westernised and eager to link his fortunes to an English scientist involved in genetic experimentation as a means of eliminating the random in life.

Monica Ali: *Brick Lane*

Monica Ali's *Brick Lane* is similarly concerned with the disappointments of a father who regards the westernisation of his children as a process of corruption. He, too, is an educated man who fails to achieve any of his ambitions; finally he concludes that he must return home to Bangladesh. His wife, knowing that their daughters can never acclimatise to life in Dhaka, concludes with some regret that she cannot leave. Her marriage has been an arranged one, she originally arrived in Tower Hamlets knowing no-one and speaking no English, her baby son has died, she has rejected a younger lover – but the real tragedy lies in the irreconcilability of these two perspectives: to go or to stay.

> 'You see,' he said, and he mumbled it inside her palm, 'All these years I dreamed of going home a Big Man. Only now, when it's nearly finished for me, I realised what is important. As long as I have my family with me, my wife, my daughters, I am strong as any man alive.'
>
> He rested his forehead on her shoulder. A sigh shook his body. She pulled him a little closer.
>
> 'What is all this Big Man?' She whispered in his ear. Sadness crushed her chest. It pressed everything out of her and filled the hollows of her bones. 'What is all this Strong Man? Do you think that is why I love you? Is that what there is in you, to be loved?'
>
> His tears scarred her hand.
>
> 'You're coming with me, then? You'll come?'
>
> 'No,' she breathed. She lifted his head and looked into his face. It was dented and swollen, almost out of recognition. 'I can't go with you,' she said.
>
> 'I can't stay,' said Chanu, and they clung to each other inside a sadness that went beyond words and tears, beyond that place, those causes and consequences, and became part of their breath, their marrow, to travel with them from now to wherever they went.

The post-colonial novels cited here do not offer a crude equation whereby life in the colonial world is wickedly oppressive and life beyond this subjection is transformed into an idyllic paradise of freedom and self-determination. Nor is London presented as a golden world of opportunity. At the end of *Small Island*, Hortense has painfully shed her illusions of English life; Queenie, her English landlady, has proved a beacon of cheerful humanity, but she is determined to part with her beautiful – black – baby because she knows that her husband and the wider world she inhabits will not accept him. *Brick Lane* concludes with sadness and defeat for Chanu, who faces a choice between exile or solitariness. But for his wife, Nazneen, who has arrived in London at the age of eighteen as 'an unspoilt girl. From the village', there are undreamed of possibilities:

> In front of her was a huge white circle, bounded by four-foot-high boards. Glinting, dazzling, enchanting ice. She looked at the ice and slowly it revealed itself. The criss-cross patterns of a thousand surface scars, the colours that shifted and changed in the lights, the unchanging nature of what lay beneath. A woman swooped by on one leg. No sequins, no short skirt. She wore jeans ...
> 'Here are your boots, Amma.'
> Nazneen turned round. To get on the ice physically – it hardly seemed to matter. In her mind she was already there.
> She said, 'But you can't skate in a sari.'
> Razia was already lacing her boots. 'This is England,' she said. 'You can do whatever you like.'

▶ Look at the extract from Andrea Levy's *Small Island* (pages 88–89) and compare the situation of Hortense with Nazneen in *Brick Lane* (above). Examine the ways in which Levy and Ali explore the conflicts that arise from cultural difference.

Plot and structure

Just as the convention of the omniscient narrator has survived into contemporary writing, so too does the convention of linear narrative. That is, the chronological structuring of events whereby the novel opens at a critical moment, proceeds through drama or crisis and reaches some sense of closure at the end of the text, the 'organisation of narrative according to a logic of causality and temporal sequence' in David Lodge's definition. It might be expected that contemporary fiction is experimental in questioning whether narrative structure can be as orderly as this linear pattern would imply. Modernist writers of the 1920s rejected conventional ideas of plot; Virginia Woolf expressed the view that the traditionally structured plot is a falsification. Her novels emphasise the randomness and lack of meaning of existence, and reject the stability of cause-and-effect, questioning whether life is experienced with apparent dependability and neatness and suggesting, rather, that existence lacks the logic of form and shape. In analysing the structure of any novel, it needs to be borne in mind that the author carefully crafts the material of the text, constantly making deliberate choices: where to begin unfolding the narrative; whether to look backwards or forwards; how to convey the impression of time passing; how much information the reader needs; what to exclude or compress. Novelist Andrew O'Hagan has said of his novel *Be Near Me* (2006) that plot is not perhaps the most interesting aspect of the text to consider; the plot is sequential but the moral drama of the work is not. Often, it is the interior world of the novel that is absorbing rather than the external world of facts and events.

Linear narrative

Ian McEwan's *Saturday* is an excellent example of a chronologically ordered narrative: the novel spans one day in the life of Henry Perowne, opening before dawn as he wakes unexpectedly and concluding as he falls into a deep sleep late at night. A random encounter in the city early in his day sets in train a series of events which will have a violently disruptive effect on his family, resulting in a climactic finale and Perowne's attempt to restore, through his professional abilities, a semblance of civilised values. In terms of the emotional lives of the characters involved, the use of retrospective narrative reveals information about Perowne's marriage, children, father-in-law. Key incidents or moments illustrate the nature of the personalities involved, as well as conveying information as to the class and culture these people represent at this moment in the 21st century. At the end of the novel, Perowne has also discovered that his daughter is pregnant, so as well as thinking about the inevitable death of his now senile mother, the novel anticipates the happy birth of new life. Perowne grumbles that he has not yet met the father of this child – an Italian archaeologist – but he is willing to embrace any plan that has 'kindness and warmth at its heart'.

But the novel is not only concerned with one day, however momentous, in the lives of these characters, it is profoundly concerned with the nature of time itself. Written in the aftermath of 9/11, yet before the London bombings of 2005, the novel is full of foreboding that time itself might be coming to a full stop: the characters – and readers – inhabit 'a community of anxiety'. Henry Perowne is an educated, liberal secularist: he doesn't believe in God, but he does believe in the values of civilised society. He knows that the health and well-being of a safe and tolerant society depend on the co-operation of its members, a fragile symbiosis. The individual human brain is, for the most part, miraculously well-ordered – his own intellect has acquired a degree of specialist expertise beyond the comprehension of the vast majority of McEwan's readers. On a different level, his daughter, threatened with the possibility of rape or murder, recalls perfectly an entire Victorian poem memorised in childhood. But his attacker Baxter's brain, with one aberrant gene, does not conform to civilised norms and will never be capable of amendment. The logic of cause-and-effect escapes him, just as, within the contemporary political climate, a view of the world as comprehensible and susceptible to rational enquiry must now be jettisoned.

The novel opens with the recollection of New York's burning towers: it forces the reader to acknowledge that the human mind is also capable of acts of violence and self-destruction on an apocalyptic scale. At the end of the text, the reader understands why McEwan has adhered to the structure of a single day: it intensifies the suspense and drama of Perowne's situation, yet emphasises the uncertainty of international events. Peace is restored to Perowne's family but peace has not yet been achieved in the wider world framing these domestic events. The 'end' cannot be known.

Barry Unsworth: *Morality Play*

Barry Unsworth's *Morality Play* (1995) plays with challenging ideas of plot and meaning: there is a spirit of rational enquiry in the novel, indeed a murder mystery will be conclusively solved. But the logic of cause-and-effect operates in an entirely different way because of the medieval context: this is a world in which human existence is both painful and mysterious, mortal life is no more than a brief interlude before death and judgement, and meaning itself belongs only to God. Unlike the contemporary world, where there is an expectation that cause-and-effect can be empirically understood, the medieval mind does not expect to grasp the meaning of things and, indeed, is taught that life is inherently mysterious and beyond human comprehension. In narrative terms, only God knows and understands the plot.

▶ Think about the way in which time is structured through any one novel you have studied. Suggest why the author has chosen to organise his or her chosen material in this way.

Structure and secrets

Authors can sometimes choose a framing device to enclose the central narrative. This has various different functions. In Sebastian Faulks' *Birdsong* the modern frame-tale acts as a bridge between the reader and the distant past of the First World War (see page 33). In certain texts the narrator himself is the framing device, looking back as the **frame narrator** at painful, perhaps imperfectly understood, experiences of childhood.

Michael Frayn: *Spies* and Louis Begley: *Wartime Lies*

Two novels to exploit this effect of emotional distance are Michael Frayn's *Spies* (2002) and Louis Begley's *Wartime Lies* (1991), both set in the context of the Second World War. In both texts an old man reflects over his very different self as a child in the war. In Frayn's novel, the young Stephen plays games of spying which uncover dark and destructive adult secrets; in Begley's work a Polish Jewish child is forced to lie about his identity to avoid inevitable death. In *Spies* an entire world of secrets is concealed behind the apparently untroubled world of a respectable suburban close: two boys invent a game that will bring about consequences they barely understand. They believe they have found a concealed German spy; in fact they have uncovered the secret of a deserter from the RAF, a man who is disastrously in love with his wife's sister. Stephen begins to see the truth of this situation rather too late to save the apparently reserved and respectable woman from the concealed sadism of her older husband. He has still less understanding that his quiet and affectionate father is both Jewish and German. Indeed, the narrator himself is not Stephen Wheatley but Stefan Weitzler, and he will, in adulthood, choose to pursue his German identity. In this text the choice of structure is appropriate to the theme itself. Stephen begins to discern the truth in childhood, but will only fully understand as an adult:

> Once again I feel the locked box beginning to open and reveal its mysteries. I'm leaving behind the old tunnels and terrors of childhood – and stepping into a new world of even darker tunnels and more elusive terrors.

At the beginning and end of the novel – the frame – Stephen returns to the streets of his childhood in search of an elusive fragrance of the past. He makes his solitary pilgrimage, although he recognises that 'the old country of the past … [will] never be reached again'.

Spies is a complex web of secrets and lies. Begley's novel is a darker evocation of a child's world, belonging to a growing genre of Holocaust literature. Here, the betrayals cause more than children's taunts or domestic tyranny. They lead to Auschwitz. Identity is denied and then lost in this tale: the frame is complicated by its literary allusions and distanced by the style of the third-person narrator. A melancholy and bookish man spends the quiet evenings of middle age with Virgil's *Aeneid*, finding in the classical tale of war the first 'civil expression for his own shame at being alive'. The references to Virgil and Dante unite the sufferings of Poland's Jews with ancient battles and the tortures of the damned in Dante's depiction of Hell. The protagonist looks back at his childhood, lived entirely in the shadow of Nazism, and the tale then unfolds in the first person. It is a story of the lies required for survival: the child who emerges from a cellar at the end has been transformed into a Polish Catholic. He has lost his name, race and, he believes, his honour: '… is Maciek's name again Maciek? Has the unmentionable Jewish family name been resumed? Certainly not … Maciek has new Aryan papers and a new Polish surname with not a whiff of the Jew in it.' As he assumes his post-war identity, the novel moves away from the first-person narrator to the distanced perspective of the third-person.

The purpose of the frame is to separate the horrifying memory of the past from the older man who seeks refuge in his reading: although he feels he is a 'voyeur of evil', he will never read of the war or the Holocaust. He has a new life and his childhood is not past in any normal way; it is repressed and concealed:

> And where is Maciek now? He became an embarrassment and slowly died. A man who bears one of the names Maciek used has replaced him. Is there much of Maciek in that man? No: Maciek was a child, and our man has no childhood that he can bear to remember; he has had to invent one.

As with *Spies*, the carefully crafted frame and subtle use of narrative make a point about deception and identity.

Structure and multi-layered narrative

The two novels discussed above present the aberrant experiences of war through the limited perception of a child. The reader is then in the position of seeing or knowing more than the central consciousness of the tale. Other writers move between different narrators and time scales and structure a complex collage of different points of view. There may be a number of different reasons for this choice of narrative structure. When the subject is war, it might be because the experience of war is so alienating – so remote from the reader's perception of 'normality' – that a seamless narrative voice cannot do justice to the enormity of the subject matter. It may, in the case of gothic or extraordinary material, be a means by which the bizarre or taboo can be presented to the reader. With post-colonial fiction, different narrators may be able to show the multicultural complexity of contemporary urban life. Zadie Smith's *White Teeth* opens on New Year's Day, 1975. It moves between the different but interlinked stories of the Iqbal and the Jones families, and ranges across the story of the two men who befriended each other during the Second World War. It travels from Kingston, Jamaica, to Willesden, London. It also explores varying degrees of Muslim religiosity, Jehovah's Witnesses and scientific atheism. In Monica Ali's *Brick Lane,* two narratives reveal the cultural differences between the lives of two sisters as well as the ironic similarities: Nazneen has come to London and will indeed choose to remain in Brick Lane rather than return to Bangladesh with her husband; her sister Hasina has remained at home where she is regarded as shockingly unorthodox in her behaviour, but she is clearly a survivor.

Kate Atkinson: *Behind the Scenes at the Museum*

The multi-layered narrative can also be a way of illuminating the dramas of unremarkable lives. Kate Atkinson's *Behind the Scenes at the Museum* (1995) begins in 1951 with the protagonist's conception and concludes in 1992 with the death of her mother. It is only towards the end of her narrative that she discovers the astonishing truth about herself and her identity. Other lives and their stories are interwoven into this chronological narrative: individuals who are frozen in time in family photographs but who have lived their own lives of love, jealousy, war and unfulfilled longings. The accumulation of these different stories has the effect of emphasising the random and unpredictable in human experience: a little girl falls through the ice, the Archduke Franz Ferdinand is shot. One event is crystallised for ever in history books; the other event is entirely insignificant except to those few persons to whom it is totally devastating. Atkinson is experimenting with the possibilities of the genre here: can the reader grasp and be interested in all these different human stories? She draws attention to historical chronology by linking the protagonist's life with key events such as the Coronation or the 1966 World Cup. At the same time she interrupts the linear pattern and achieves an effect of simultaneity, as though all her 20th-century stories exist in the same time frame.

Closure

Closure is a term used loosely (and frequently) nowadays to identify a satisfactory conclusion to a troubling event: for example, people might be said to achieve 'closure' after being the victims of a crime when the criminal is caught and punished. However, it is also the technical term used to discuss and analyse the conclusion to a text. It might be expected that, in contemporary fiction, closure is not necessarily a simple matter of the chief characters living 'happily ever after'. As with titles, openings and narrators, the end of a text is consciously shaped. The author might be seen in the light of a film director who spends some time considering the final image he or she wishes to leave in the mind of the viewer. There are novels that conclude positively – even defiantly – despite what seem like unresolvable problems and uncertainties. *Brick Lane* is an excellent example: Nazneen and her husband have irreconcilable views of life despite a genuine love for each other, and Ali ends the novel on a liberating note with Nazneen joyously ice-skating in her sari. Often, though, a contemporary text will end in uncertainty: Andrew O' Hagan's *Be Near Me* (2006) concludes with Father David, the now-disgraced priest, visiting the husband of his former housekeeper Mrs Poole, at Christmas. Mr Poole is a man who is widowed and alone, drinking his way through the regrets of his first Christmas without his wife. At the end of this awkward social encounter, David leaves – but the reader has no idea where he is going. It is a freezing December evening in Scotland, his life in the Church is now presumably over, he has sacrificed what vocation he possessed for a brief, impulsive abandonment to desire. Factually, the reader knows nothing; the language suggests symbolically the possibility of journeying on, a new direction:

> On reaching the top of the [railway] bridge he was happy to observe he was nothing much, just another person looking for faith in the cold night air. A goods train came and he watched its iron trucks go by, until there was only the cloud of his breath and the small red lights at the back of the train, the lights getting smaller and then flaring just once as it vanished into the trees.

Where a novel has been concerned throughout with a central relationship, it would seem perverse to conclude the text with no real sense of whether or not this partnership will survive. Yet this is the case with McEwan's *Enduring Love*. The narrator, Joe, is happily in love with Clarissa and their world appears entirely settled until Joe becomes haunted by the increasingly threatening and obsessive Parry. After a violently explosive climax to this claustrophobic situation, Clarissa announces by letter that they must, if only temporarily, part:

> A stranger invaded our lives, and the first thing that happened was that you became a stranger to me. You worked out he had de Clérambault's syndrome (if that really is a disease) … [but] why it happened, how it changed you, how it might have been otherwise, what it did to us – that's what we've got now, and that's what we have to think about … I don't know where this takes us. We've been so happy together. We've loved each other passionately and loyally. I always thought our love was the kind that was meant to go on and on. Perhaps it will. I just don't know.

In the final chapter, they return together to Oxford to clarify a minor mystery which has run through the novel; this may unite them in some way, but no certainty is offered. McEwan concludes with a small child requesting Joe to repeat his earlier conversational image of the individual atoms of the river stretching out infinitely towards the sea. Unlike O'Hagan's novel, this is not a metaphor that offers elucidation. Have Clarissa and Joe been separated forever? The text itself moves outside the 'story' to include psychiatric discussion of de Clérambault's syndrome and a case history of 'P' which closely resembles the material of the novel. Here, too, a relationship is strained by the pressure of events, but the reader is informed starkly, 'they separated'. Is this intended to shed light on Joe and Clarissa, or is McEwan suggesting that there is an unknown future, beyond the scope of the text? It is certainly a matter for the reader's individual interpretation.

Similarly, the marriage of Ralph and Anna in Hilary Mantel's *A Change of Climate* seems doomed: Ralph is actually leaving their home with suitcases and Anna has consulted her lawyer. But at the moment of departure, a despairing and loveless human being crawls towards them and together they move towards her, reaching out to rescue her. The novelist does not go beyond this instinct on their part, however, and the novel ends with Ralph's sister, Emma, making a return visit to the shrine of Walsingham to pray for the family. As she leaves, a cold and watery sun fitfully appears from behind the clouds 'like a lamp behind a veil'. Is the imagery intended to encourage optimism? Again, the reader must decide.

Coetzee's *Disgrace*, unsurprisingly given the uncompromising nature of the novel, is peculiarly bleak in its ending. David Lurie assists the unattractive but worthy Bev Shaw in her animal welfare work: on Sundays they mercifully destroy the maimed or unwanted dogs that cannot be cared for. This is an unremittingly miserable business – in the context of Coetzee's South Africa, life is cheap and there is no one to care for unwanted animals. Like his daughter Lucy, David has been reduced to starting again with nothing. What he recognises here – that he had failed to see before – is that Bev's mission is not to be despised or mocked:

> One by one Bev touches them, speaks to them, comforts them, and puts them away … He and Bev do not speak. He has learned by now, from her, to concentrate all his attention on the animal they are killing, giving it what he no longer has difficulty in calling by its proper name: love.

► Contemporary novels often end in uncertain and seemingly inconclusive ways. Examine the endings of one or more contemporary novels, discussing their effectiveness in the light of the novel as a whole.

Character

What exactly is 'character' in the novel? This seemingly obvious question has been the source of much critical debate. Assumptions about 'rounded' or 'flat' characters have largely been discarded, and it is some time since examination questions would simply invite 'character discussion'. Critical theorists reject as invalid any attempt to discuss Shakespearean and other characters as if they were real people, rather than the creations of the imagination. Many critics would also question how far textual analysis should focus on single characters rather than considering the world they represent. The French theoretical writer Jean-François Lyotard, for example, suggests:

> A *self* does not amount to much, but no self is an island; each exists in a fabric of revelations that is now more complex and mobile than ever before.

It might be argued that this is an extreme view: just as novels continue to be written, published and enthusiastically received and discussed, so too does the concept of literary characterisation. Readers talk about novels and part of this discourse will inevitably be some discussion of the characters of the text. There is no doubt, however, that the portrayal of character, as well as the concept of what character is, has altered significantly from its portrayal by, say, Victorian writers such as Dickens. Indeed, the centrality of character has shifted, just as other stable certainties (both textual and philosophical) have been questioned. To call up the great novels of the 19th century is to enumerate classic texts where the novel is the eponymous hero or heroine: *Emma, Jane Eyre, David Copperfield, Anna Karenina, Madame Bovary*, or, at the extreme limits of imaginative fancy, *Frankenstein, Dr Jekyll and Mr Hyde, Dracula*. The reader is being invited to enter a fully realised individual world, to view the universe through the perspective of this specific individual. It would be difficult now to cite so many highly regarded works titled with the name of an eponymous hero or heroine. The closest equivalent among the texts discussed here would be Ondaatje's *The English Patient*, where the title *does* allude to the central personality of the text, but in a riddling way since he is a Hungarian Count, Lázló de Almásy. As John Mullan observes in his study, *How Novels Work*, the novel could not exist without its people:

> Nothing is stranger or more important in our reading of novels than the sense that we are encountering real people in them.

Pat Barker: *Regeneration*

Pat Barker's *Regeneration* trilogy is an excellent illustration. The novels involve historical characters such as Wilfred Owen and Siegfried Sassoon, but are structured around the fictional Billy Prior who unites all three novels. He appears as one of Rivers' patients at Craiglockhart in *Regeneration* and concludes *The Ghost Road*, where he dies with Owen days before the end of the war. Billy Prior is far more than a narrative device though: he is angry, defiant, vibrantly alive. He pursues his bisexual affairs with energy, despises the Army's typical upper-class officer, refuses to respond to the patient tolerance of Rivers and neatly turns the tables on him in one of their exchanges:

> 'I suppose it's just a matter of officers having a more complex mental life.'
> Prior reacted as though he'd been stung. 'Are you serious? You honestly believe that that *gaggle* of noodle-brained half-wits down there has a complex mental life? Oh, *Rivers*.'
> 'I'm not saying it's *universally* true, only that it's *generally* true. Simply as a result of officers receiving a different and, for the most part, more prolonged education.'
> '*The public schools.*'
> ...
> Prior smiled.

'You know one day you're going to have to accept the fact that you're in this hospital because you're ill. Not me. Not the CO. Not the kitchen porter. *You.*'

After Prior had gone, Rivers sat for a while, half amused, half irritated ... Bugger Prior, he thought.

Prior is, in part, a means by which the events of the war can be made more vivid. The reader may know generally of conditions in the trenches and, specifically, of Wilfred Owen's death in the final days of the war, but Prior has the ability to shock. There is no pathos in his death, rather his own defiant scepticism. He keeps a diary, as do many of the soldiers around him. Letters and poems abound, about which Prior has evolved his own theory:

Why? you have to ask yourself. I think it's a way of claiming immunity. First-person narrators can't die, so as long as we keep telling the story of our own lives we're safe. Ha bloody fucking Ha.

So, in Barker's trilogy, historical as it is, the character of Prior is a crucial means by which the reader's attention is seized and engaged. Prior is the way in which history is made into fictional narrative.

▶ Look at any one contemporary novel you have studied, in the light of the author's methods of characterisation. Have you found anything innovative or challenging here?

Character as subject: *The Woman Who Walked into Doors*

Roddy Doyle's *The Woman Who Walked into Doors* (1996) is one of the rare contemporary novels that proclaims the heroine's centrality in its title, although it is a dark, even sardonic, means of obscuring her identity. Paula Spencer feels that she is an invisible woman, a ghost. She is beaten, wounded, bleeding; yet doctors, priests, strangers, her own parents, never enquire about her circumstances, they simply look away or assume that her own drinking is to blame. She is victimised by her husband, Charlo, to the extent that he even asks about her wounds as a way of tormenting her:

Where'd you get that?
What?
The eye.
It was a test. I was thumping inside. He was playing with me. There was only one right answer.
I walked into the door.
Is that right?
Yeah.
Looks sore.
It's not too bad.
Good.

The novel is written as a first-person narrative, so Paula's thoughts and feelings are conveyed directly to the reader. As the extract above illustrates, speech is immediate, as if a drama is unfolding. Doyle's narrative structure is highly effective in bringing the entirety of Paula's existence simultaneously to life. The reader knows early in the novel that Charlo is dead, then Paula's childhood and her courtship with Charlo unfold at the same time as her account of her attempt to create an ordered world for her children and her struggle to overcome alcoholism. Paula's early experiences are characterised by an attempt to believe that her life has value, that her father is not sadistic, that her family life is secure and happy. Her recollection of her honeymoon is juxtaposed against her troubled visualising of the murder Charlo has committed and his subsequent death, as though she must account for the fact that the optimistic and exuberant person she loved and married is the same as the man who shot an innocent woman in cold blood. This is the climax of the novel. Paula has always made excuses for Charlo's domestic violence because she is the invisible woman and no one has ever defended her. It is therefore all her own fault. But now he has both hit and killed a defenceless, grandmotherly woman alone in her own home. That would mean that Charlo is wicked, a fact she has never confronted; to do so is to face the possibility that she has always hidden behind a series of delusions:

> I loved him with all my heart. He was so kind. He just lost his temper sometimes. He loved me. He bought me things. He bought me clothes. Why didn't I wear them? Whack. But why did he whack poor Mrs Fleming? He wasn't married to her. He hit her twice. What had happened?
> I wanted none of the answers that started to breathe in me; I smothered them. They were all horrible. They were all just savage and brutal. Nasty and sick. They mocked my marriage; my love; they mocked my whole life.

This is a novel that could easily be characterised as a 'single-issue' work: domestic violence within a cultural context that denies that it exists. But Doyle has achieved far more in the portrait of Paula Spencer: she has unstoppable vitality and tenacity – she loves, dreams, survives with a wry humour, despite being systematically destroyed. The novel concludes with her satisfaction that she has thrown Charlo out of the house; once he looks speculatively at their eldest daughter, Paula asserts herself decisively in order to protect her child: 'I'd done something good'. This would seem closure indeed, so it is interesting to observe that, ten years after publication, a sequel entitled *Paula Spencer* has appeared.

The reader's judgement

Discussion of character will often raise the question of whether or not the reader likes a particular fictional character. How far is this a relevant consideration? Clearly the author must succeed in creating character and situation that, together, engage the reader's interest throughout the novel. But it may be that there is no straightforward process of empathetic involvement; rather an open-ended portrayal of a situation which requires the individual reader to form a conclusion. Coetzee's *Disgrace* is a fine example of a novel where readers probably judge David Lurie, initially, as an egotistical individual who is emotionally sterile. By the end of the text he has demonstrated an ability to look at himself with a degree of honesty and to connect with the radically different world in which he now finds himself. Here, the author portrays a character's capacity to change in thought and feeling, an ability to confront failings. Readers will inevitably differ in their judgement of Lurie according to their own situation; differences of race and gender are part of the substance of the text itself.

The novelist Andrew O'Hagan offers a telling insight into the relationship between reader and character, questioning why a central character should be likeable and suggesting that the reader might understand more of the protagonist's moral landscape than the character himself. O'Hagan's *Be Near Me* is a novel where the protagonist, Father David, is an aloof, Oxford-educated priest stranded in a challenging working-class area of West Scotland. Father David is an aesthete who cares for classical music, fine wines, French poetry – and eventually a lively teenager whom he befriends. But he appears to have little commitment to his faith or his mission as a priest, and he is snobbish with both his parishioners and fellow priests. When his actions cause real crisis, he is remote and unresponsive. Like Coetzee's David Lurie, he will not comply with the recommendations of those around him and exonerate himself from suspicion. At the end of the novel, Father David has lost position and respect; he has very little left to him. O'Hagan, in interview, has said that the reader perceives the priest's situation more clearly than the character himself. How then is the conclusion to the novel to be judged? Is it optimistic or pessimistic? The author offers no clues, but allows the individual reader to decide.

Critics of the novel now tend to place readers at the centre of critical activity. Although this was not the case until the latter end of the 20th century, there is now widespread acceptance that reader-response is crucial to the discussion of contemporary fictional writing. Novelist and critic David Lodge has said of the process of writing a novel that when 'the novel is published and goes out of your control to modify it, it also goes out of your control to intend the meaning of it'. Lodge is arguing that not even the author has the last word in interpretation.

3 | Texts and extracts

The extracts that follow have been chosen to illustrate the key themes and points made elsewhere in the book, and to provide material which may be useful when working on the assignments. The items are arranged alphabetically, with the exception of the opening piece.

Granta

Granta is a literary journal which has been prescient in identifying new talent and publishing the work of young writers. It is also an important voice in debates on the status of the novel. Here, in one of its earliest editions, an American writer gives his views on the limitations of British writing in 1980. Then Lorna Sage, critic and novelist, presents her sense that the novel is becoming revitalised by new, 'other' voices. Finally, Ian Jack, as Editor and Booker Prize judge, 1996, defines the novel as he sees it at that particular time, identifying a 'valedictory realism' as characteristic of the fiction of the end of the 20th century.

From *Granta* (1980)

> What strikes an expatriate most about the contemporary British novel is its conformity, its traditional sameness, and its realistically rendered provincialism. Shaped only by its contents, the British novel is the product of group mentality: local, quaint, and self-consciously xenophobic. Why is it that of the many able craftsmen writing in Britain so few have experimented with form, and, of those, experimented with such caution? There is no reason special to the novel genre itself. There are, however, properties about its form – an expression of a particular relation between art and life – which reveal the assumptions and beliefs underlying the characteristic narrowness of the British novel. The culture from which British fiction derives, and the culture insistently expressed in its writing, is clearly oriented towards fact, content, metonymy, empiricism, and the body.
>
> (Frederick Bowers 'An Irrelevant Parochialism', *Granta*, 1980)

> The most exciting writers now are those who have been 'invaded', and who are 'haunted' in the manner of Doris Lessing's mad ladies by voices from other continents and alternative worlds. Obviously it's not merely a formal matter, but connected with what is known euphemistically as 'Britain's Changing Place in the World' (Britain, note, not England) … What I've wanted to stress is that if the English novel in the years after the war appeared to be strangling in its own

decorous and unappetising repressions – and I'm not sure it did – it's not that way now. Instead, the direction is centrifugal. (Another way of putting it is that the world the *language* colonised is breaking in: Nadine Gordimer's Africa, for instance, or Ruth Prawer Jhabvala's India, which are indeed in some ways English.) My line is that enormous changes have taken place in what it means to be English, and that you'd expect the novel to reflect on them, even if not comfortably or quickly or very directly. I have perhaps slightly dodged my brief in not talking about comparisons with writing elsewhere, but then I am arguing that much of what's significant in English fiction is written with 'elsewhere' very much in mind; is, in a sense, written *from* elsewhere.

(Lorna Sage 'Invasion from Outsiders', *Granta*, 1980)

As one of the judges for the 1996 Booker Prize, I was struck by how many new English novels (and new English novelists) were preoccupied with the past; not with history – they weren't historical novels by way of research and period detail – but with the country and people that seemed to be there a minute ago, before we blinked and turned away. Nor were they nostalgic or romantic or (thank God) illustrative, dynastic stories of English society, comparing and contrasting the life of Family X decade by decade. Many were fine novels using new devices … How to describe this writing? Twenty years ago the Scottish writer Tom Nairn [invented] a phrase for the novels of Walter Scott. Nairn quoted the Hungarian Georg Lukács to argue that Scott was not the Romantic he is usually taken for. He belonged to a newly industrializing society and a country – Britain – that was forging a unified identity; as a writer he used the fresh tool of realism to depict another way of life in another kind of country – pre-industrial pre-British Scotland – that had only recently disappeared. He was, in Nairn's phrase, a valedictory realist.

Valedictory realism can't, of course, be confined to England or English writers; nor do writers fit neatly under such a label. In this issue the Irish writer John Banville has been inspired by a singular life – that of the English spy Sir Anthony Blunt, the keeper of the Queen's Pictures, who was publicly exposed and disgraced as a traitor during Mrs Thatcher's first year as prime minister. But that life grew among other lives … in a different, patrician England. The surface shone; the rot was underneath.

When did we say goodbye to it? Oh, it seems only yesterday. This is the literature of farewell.

(Ian Jack Editorial, *Granta*, 1996)

Angela Carter

From *Wise Children* (1991)

This is an exuberant novel, celebrating all that is comic in Shakespeare's theatre: twins, coincidences of birth, mistaken identities, as well as a relish for puns and bawdy. Dora and Nora Chance are the illegitimate twin daughters of a noble Shakespearean actor, Melchior Hazard; their theatrical destiny is in the world of music hall rather than tragic soliloquy. The young twins are stagestruck from birth; in this extract they achieve modest stardom from their Shakespearean act.

We were eighteen years old, hair like patent leather, legs up to our ears. We sported bellhop costumes for our *Hamlet* skit; should, we pondered in unison and song, the package be delivered to, I kid you not, '2b or not 2b'. We performed a syncopated Highland fling in tasselled sporrans after, as weird sisters, we burst out of a giant haggis in a number based on the banquet scene; in abbreviated togas, led the chorus during the 'Roman scandals' number; I sang my solo 'O Mistress Mine' in fifteenth-century drag to a mutely mutinous Nora on a balcony – she got the last laugh when she poured a bucket of water over me, and I didn't have much of a voice, anyway, but Mr Piano Man was besotted; we did a Morris dance with bells upon our ankles, then sang, 'it was a lover and his lass' in harmony and parts ('Hey nonny bloody no'); and went through a spirited version of the Egyptian sand dance on the deck of a large gilded barge that glided slowly from one side of the stage to the other in the spectacular conclusion of the first part of the show.

Our frocks were sumptuous. No short-cuts, no half-measures – real silk, real satin, real feathers, sequins by the truckload. There's a lot of conspicuous consumption in show business. Even the backdrops were awesome. There was a mural copied from the British Museum for the *Cleopatra* number, a bit of a John Martin behind *Macbeth*.

…

You know the song about the girl who 'danced with a man who danced with a girl who danced with the Prince of Wales'? I was the original girl. Nora, too. He couldn't tell the difference any more than anyone else could.

He dearly loved to tango. He'd have tangoed all night, if he could. He'd tango on remorselessly for a good half-hour at a time, it was a real test of your stamina. The band had to go on playing as long as he could keep it up, since he was royalty, but a tango normally lasts just the four minutes so it was as much of an ordeal as anything, especially if you'd done two shows and a matinée already. We preferred to do it in the afternoons, at the Ritz, tango teas, after they brought in dancing in the restaurant. I once picked up a flea at the Ritz in the Marie Antoinette Suite but that was later on, during the war, when I was entertaining the Free French.

J.M. Coetzee

From *Disgrace* (1999)

Coetzee is a South African writer who confronts the unresolved pain and conflict of post-apartheid society. In this novel, David Lurie, a white, middle-aged lecturer, has had a brief and tawdry affair with one of his students. Exiled from his university, he retreats to the country where his daughter, Lucy, lives alone, caring for abandoned dogs and tending the flowers and vegetables that are her livelihood. A brutal attack on them both forces him to reconsider himself and the world they inhabit. Here, towards the end of the novel, he drives to his daughter's farm: they have been 'bitterly apart' as a result of her refusal to report the savage violation upon her and her decision to persevere with the resulting pregnancy.

From the last hillcrest the farm opens out before him: the old house, solid as ever, the stables, Petrus's new house, the old dam on which he can make out specks that must be the ducks and larger specks that must be the wild geese, Lucy's visitors from afar.

At this distance the flowerbeds are solid blocks of colour: magenta, carnelian, ash-blue. A season of blooming. The bees must be in their seventh heaven.

Of Petrus there is no sign, nor of his wife or the jackal boy who runs with them. But Lucy is at work among the flowers; and, as he picks his way down the hillside, he can see the bulldog too, a patch of fawn on the path beside her.

He reaches the fence and stops. Lucy, with her back to him, has not yet noticed him. She is wearing a pale summer dress, boots, and a wide straw hat. As she bends over, clipping or pruning or tying, he can see the milky, blue-veined skin and broad, vulnerable tendons of the backs of her knees: the least beautiful part of a woman's body, the least expressive, and therefore perhaps the most endearing.

Lucy straightens up, stretches, bends down again. Field-labour; peasant tasks, immemorial. His daughter is becoming a peasant.

Still, she is not aware of him. As for the watchdog, the watchdog appears to be snoozing.

So: once she was only a little tadpole in her mother's body, and now here she is, solid in her existence, more solid than he has ever been. With luck, she will last a long time, long beyond him. When he is dead she will, with luck, still be here doing her ordinary tasks among the flowerbeds. And from within her will have issued another existence, that with luck will be just as solid, just as long-lasting. So it will go on, a line of existences, in which his share, his gift will grow inexorably less and less, till it may as well be forgotten.

A grandfather. A Joseph. Who would have thought it! What pretty girl can he expect to be wooed into bed with a grandfather?

Softly he speaks her name. 'Lucy!'

She does not hear him.

What will it entail, being a grandfather? As a father he has not been much of a success, despite trying harder than most. As a grandfather he will probably score lower than average too. He lacks the virtues of the old: equanimity, kindliness, patience. But perhaps those virtues will come as other virtues go: the virtue of passion, for instance. He must have a look again at Victor Hugo, poet of grandfatherhood. There may be things to learn.

The wind drops. There is a moment of utter stillness which he would wish prolonged for ever: the gentle sun, the stillness of mid-afternoon, bees busy in a field of flowers; and at the centre of the picture a young woman, *das ewig Weibliche*, lightly pregnant, in a straw sunhat. A scene ready-made for a Sargent or a Bonnard. City boys like him; but even city boys can recognize beauty when they see it, can have their breath taken away.

The truth is, he has never had much of an eye for rural life, despite all his reading in Wordsworth. Not much of an eye for anything, except pretty girls; and where has that got him? Is it too late to educate the eye?

He clears his throat. 'Lucy,' he says, more loudly.

The spell is broken. Lucy comes erect, half-turns, smiles. 'Hello,' she says. 'I didn't hear you.'

Katy raises her head and stares short-sightedly in his direction.

He clambers through the fence. Katy lumbers up to him, sniffs his shoes.

'Where is the truck?' asks Lucy. She is flushed from her labours and perhaps a little sunburnt. She looks, suddenly, the picture of health.

'I parked and took a walk.'

'Will you come in and have some tea?'

She makes the offer as if he were a visitor. Good. Visitorship, visitation: a new footing, a new start.

Kazuo Ishiguro

From *Never Let Me Go* (2005)

In this bleak and disturbing novel, Kathy H looks back over her childhood at Hailsham, an establishment deep in the countryside for 'special' individuals. The children are cared for, indeed encouraged to pursue artistic activities, but gradually they become aware that they are 'different' and that society has destined them for a brief life and an inescapably brutal end. In this extract, Kathy recalls an innocent moment from childhood, singing along with her cassette tape-player; she becomes aware, though, that the adult gaze directed at her contains a freight of meaning she does not yet comprehend.

There was one strange incident around this time I should tell you about here. It really unsettled me, and although I wasn't to find out its real meaning until years later, I think I sensed, even then, some deeper significance to it.

It was a sunny afternoon and I'd gone to our dorm to get something. I remember how bright it was because the curtains in our room hadn't been pulled back properly, and you could see the sun coming in in big shafts and see all the dust in the air. I hadn't meant to play the tape, but since I was there all by myself, an impulse made me get the cassette out of my collection box and put it into the player.

Maybe the volume had been turned right up by whoever had been using it last, I don't know. But it was much louder than I usually had it and that was probably why I didn't hear her before I did. Or maybe I'd just got complacent by then. Anyway, what I was doing was swaying about slowly in time to the song, holding an imaginary baby to my breast. In fact, to make it all the more embarrassing, it was one of those times I'd grabbed a pillow to stand in for the baby, and I was doing this slow dance, my eyes closed, singing along softly each time those lines came round again:

'Oh baby, *baby*, never let me go ...'

The song was almost over when something made me realise I wasn't alone, and I opened my eyes to find myself staring at Madame framed in the doorway.

I froze in shock. Then within a second or two, I began to feel a new kind of alarm, because I could see there was something strange about the situation. The door was almost half open – it was a sort of rule we couldn't close dorm doors completely except for when we were sleeping – but Madame hadn't nearly come up to the threshold. She was out in the corridor, standing very still, her head angled to one side to give her a view of what I was doing inside. And the odd thing was she was crying. It might even have been one of her sobs that had come through the song to jerk me out of my dream.

When I think about this now, it seems to me, even if she wasn't a guardian, she was the adult, and she should have said or done something, even if it was just to tell me off. Then I'd have known how to behave. But she just went on standing out there, sobbing and sobbing, staring at me through the doorway with that same look in her eyes she always had when she looked at us, like she was seeing something that gave her the creeps. Except this time there was something else, something extra in that look I couldn't fathom.

Andrea Levy

From *Small Island* (2004)

Small Island interweaves the post-war experiences of Hortense, who leaves her native Jamaica to join her husband Gilbert in London, with Queenie Bligh their young landlady. Hortense has arrived in England with fantasies of adopting the elegant and refined lifestyle of the 'Mother Country'. She is shocked to encounter a drab and restrictive post-war world, and unprepared for racial incomprehension and prejudice. Yet she is a spirited individual, determined that she will achieve the golden future once predicted for her. In this encounter, from the end of the novel, Hortense and Gilbert have been asked to adopt Queenie's baby, the result of a brief wartime affair between Queenie and a Jamaican airman.

Mr Bligh stepped back one stride, not in fear of Gilbert but only so he might better show his disdain by perusing him up and down. 'Why, in God's name, would Queenie think to entrust the baby's upbringing to people like you? That poor little half-caste child would be better off begging in a gutter!' he said.

Gilbert sucked on his teeth to return this man's scorn. 'You know what your trouble is, man?' he said. 'Your white skin. You think it makes you better than me. You think it give you the right to lord it over a black man. But you know what it make you? You wan' know what your white skin make you, man? It make you white. That is all, man. White. No better, no worse than me – just white.' Mr Bligh moved his eye to gaze on the ceiling. 'Listen to me, man, we both just finish fighting a war – a bloody war – for the better world we wan' see. And on the same side – you and me. We both look on other men to see enemy. You and me, fighting for empire, fighting for peace. But still, after all that we suffer together, you wan' tell me I am worthless and you are not. Am I to be the servant and you are the master for all time? No. Stop this, man. Stop it now. We can work together, Mr Bligh. You no see? We must. Or else you just gonna fight me till the end?'

Gilbert had hushed the room. It was not only Mr Bligh whose mouth gaped in wonder. Even the baby had fallen silent. For at that moment as Gilbert stood, his chest panting with the passion from his words, I realised that Gilbert Joseph, my husband, was a man of class, a man of character, a man of intelligence. Noble in a way that would some day make him a legend. 'Gilbert Joseph', everyone would shout. 'Have you heard about Gilbert Joseph?'

And Mr Bligh, blinking straight in Gilbert's eye once more, said softly, 'I'm sorry'. Of course, I thought, of course. Who would not be chastened by those fine words from my smart, handsome and noble husband? But this Englishman just carried on, 'I'm sorry … but I just can't understand a single word that you're saying.'

Gilbert's august expression slipped from his face to shatter into tiny pieces upon the floor. He leaned down to me and took the baby from my arms. Straightening himself he handed the bundled baby to Mr Bligh. He then took my hand in his and guided me silently from the room.

Ian McEwan

From *Saturday* (2005)

The novel follows Henry Perowne, successful neurosurgeon, through a single Saturday, a day which, from dawn, appears full of unpredictable menace. As London's streets are teeming with anti-war protestors, a chance encounter threatens Henry's closest family. This extract is taken from the opening of the novel. Henry has woken unexpectedly and looks out of his window at the familiar London square around him; gradually he becomes aware that an inexplicable light in the sky is not a distant comet but a plane, on fire.

He's moving towards the bed when he hears a low rumbling sound, gentle thunder gathering in volume, and stops to listen. It tells him everything. He looks back over his shoulder to the window for confirmation. Of course, a comet is so distant it's bound to appear stationary. Horrified, he returns to his position by the window. The sound holds at a steady volume, while he revises the scale again, zooming inwards this time, from solar dust and ice back to the local. Only three or four seconds have passed since he saw this fire in the sky and changed his mind about it twice. It's travelling along a route that he himself has taken many times in his life, and along which he's gone through the routines, adjusting his seat-back and his watch, putting away his papers, always curious to see if he can locate his own house down among the immense almost beautiful orange-grey sprawl; east to west, along the southern banks of the Thames, two thousand feet up, in the final approaches to Heathrow.

It's directly south of him now, barely a mile away, soon to pass into the topmost lattice of the bare plane trees, and then behind the Post Office Tower, at the level of the lowest microwave dishes. Despite the city lights, the contours of the plane aren't visible in the early-morning darkness. The fire must be on the nearside wing where it joins the fuselage, or perhaps in one of the engines slung below. The leading edge of the fire is a flattened white sphere which trails away in a cone of yellow and red, less like a meteor or comet than an artist's lurid impression of one. As though in a pretence of normality, the landing lights are flashing. But the engine note gives it all away. Above the usual deep and airy roar, is a straining, choking, banshee sound growing in volume – both a scream and a sustained shout, an impure, dirty noise that suggests unsustainable mechanical effort beyond the capacity of hardened steel, spiralling upwards to an end point, irresponsibly rising and rising like the accompaniment to a terrible fairground ride. Something is about to give.

He no longer thinks of waking Rosalind. Why wake her into this nightmare? In fact, the spectacle has the familiarity of a recurrent dream. Like most passengers, outwardly subdued by the monotony of air travel, he often lets his thoughts range across the possibilities while sitting, strapped down and docile, in front of a packaged meal. Outside, beyond a wall of thin steel and cheerful creaking plastic, it's minus sixty degrees and forty thousand feet to the ground. Flung across the Atlantic at five hundred feet a second, you submit to the folly because everyone else does. Your fellow passengers are reassured because you and the others around you appear calm. Looked at a certain way – deaths per passenger mile – the statistics are consoling. And how else attend a conference in Southern California? Air travel is a stock market, a trick of mirrored perceptions, a fragile alliance of pooled belief; so long as nerves hold steady and no bombs or wreckers are on board, everybody prospers. When there's failure, there will be no half measures. Seen another way – deaths per journey – the figures aren't so good. The market could plunge.

Plastic fork in hand, he often wonders how it might go – the screaming in the cabin partly muffled by that deadening acoustic, the fumbling in bags for phones and last words, the airline staff in their terror clinging to remembered fragments of procedure, the levelling smell of shit. But the scene construed from the outside, from afar like this, is also familiar. It's already almost eighteen months since half the planet watched, and watched again the unseen captives driven through the sky to the slaughter, at which time there gathered around the innocent silhouette of any jet plane a novel association. Everyone agrees, airliners look different in the sky these days, predatory or doomed.

Michael Ondaatje

From *The English Patient* (1992)

The Second World War is nearing its end in Europe, and a burned and unrecognisable man is dying in a ruined Italian villa, attended by a nurse, Hana, and the memories of a fateful love affair. As the narrative unfolds, the reader becomes aware that the protagonist's fascination with the desert is inextricably linked with his tragedy. In this extract, the protagonist's chosen book, from which he cannot be parted, is Herodotus' histories – accounts of ancient warfare. His companion, Madox, cannot reconcile the silence and beauty of the desert with the chaos and hypocrisy of war.

> I, Herodotus of Halicarnassus, set forth my history, that time may not draw the colour from what Man has brought into being, nor those great and wonderful deeds manifested by both Greeks and Barbarians ... together with the reason they fought one another.

Men had always been the reciters of poetry in the desert. And Madox – to the Geographical Society – had spoken beautiful accounts of our traversals and coursings. Bermann blew theory into the embers. And I? I was the skill among them. The mechanic. The others wrote out their love of solitude and meditated on what they found there. They were never sure of what I thought of it all. 'Do you like that moon?' Madox asked me after he'd known me for ten years. He asked it tentatively, as if he had breached an intimacy. For them I was a bit too cunning to be a lover of the desert. More like Odysseus. Still, I was. Show me a desert, as you would show another man a river, or another man the metropolis of his childhood.

... When we parted for the last time, Madox used the old farewell. 'May God make safety your companion.' And I strode away from him saying, 'There is no God.' We were utterly unlike each other.

Madox said Odysseus never wrote a word, an intimate book. Perhaps he felt alien in the false rhapsody of art. And my own monograph, I must admit, had been stern with accuracy. The fear of describing her presence as I wrote caused me to burn down all sentiment, all rhetoric of love. Still, I described the desert as purely as I would have spoken of her. Madox asked me about the moon during our last days together before the war began. We parted. He left for England, the probability of the oncoming war interrupting everything, our slow unearthing of history in the desert. Good-bye, Odysseus, he said, grinning, knowing I was never that fond of Odysseus, less fond of Aeneas, but we had decided Bagnold was Aeneas. But I was not that fond of Odysseus either. Good-bye, I said.

I remember he turned back, laughing ... He returned to his wife in the village of Marston Magna, took only his favourite volume of Tolstoy, left all of his compasses and maps to me. Our affection left unspoken.

And Marston Magna in Somerset, which he had evoked for me again and again in our conversations, had turned its green fields into an aerodrome. The planes burned their exhaust over Arthurian castles. What drove him to the act I do not know. Maybe it was the permanent noise of flight, so loud to him now after the simple drone of the Gypsy Moth that had putted over our silences in Libya and Egypt. Someone's war was slashing apart his delicate tapestry of companions. I was Odysseus, I understood the shifting and temporary vetoes of war. But he was a man who made friends with difficulty. He was a man who knew two or three people in his life, and they had turned out now to be the enemy.

He was in Somerset alone with his wife, who had never met us. Small gestures were enough for him. One bullet ended the war.

It was July 1939. They caught a bus from their village into Yeovil. The bus had been slow and so they had been late for the service. At the back of the crowded church, in order to find seats they decided to sit separately. When the sermon began half an hour later, it was jingoistic and without any doubt in its support of the war. The priest intoned blithely about battle, blessing the government and the men about to enter the war. Madox listened as the sermon grew more impassioned. He pulled out the desert pistol, bent over and shot himself in the heart. He was dead immediately. A great silence. Desert silence. Planeless silence. They heard his body collapse against the pew. Nothing else moved. The priest frozen in a gesture. It was like those silences when a glass funnel round a candle in church splits and all faces turn. His wife walked down the centre aisle, stopped at his row, muttered something, and they let her in beside him. She knelt down, her arms enclosing him.

Jane Smiley

From *A Thousand Acres* (1991)

This is a novel which is based on Shakespeare's *King Lear*: in Jane Smiley's own words, '... the ideas about Lear's daughters and about agriculture had been knocking around in my mind for fifteen years or so, but the exact moment they jelled was when I was driving down I-35 in northern Iowa in late March 1988. The landscape was flat and cold, lit by a weak winter sun, and as I stared out the window, the farm fields seemed enormous and isolated. As soon as I said, "This is where I could set that Lear book," the whole thing came into my mind, and the image of that bleak landscape remained throughout the writing of the book as a talisman to return to every time composition faltered.'

The tragedy unfolds with painful inevitability; it is a tale which stands alone, but gains in intensity from even a basic knowledge of *Lear*. In this extract, an elderly farmer has divided his land between his daughters, but has come to resent this, feeling increasingly embittered at his now redundant role. As he curses his two elder daughters, a storm rages, corresponding with the scene at the centre of the play where Lear is turned out into the stormy night.

A pair of headlights turned off the road, momentarily crossed the back wall of the room, went dark. Rose stayed where she was and didn't say anything. I sat still. After a long, quiet moment, punctuated by the bang bang of two truck doors closing, Ty's voice, low and calm, said, 'Ginny, come out here please.'

This was it.

Rose pushed the screen door and I followed her. Our father was standing in front of the truck. Ty was behind him. He said, 'Larry has some things to say. I told him he should tell you them himself.'

Daddy said, 'That's right.'

Rose took my hand and squeezed it, as she had often done when we were kids, and in trouble, waiting for punishment.

Daddy said, resentfully, 'That's right. Hold hands.'

I said, 'Why shouldn't we? All we've ever really had is each other. Anyway, what are we in trouble for? Why are you getting ready to tell us a bunch of things? We haven't done anything wrong except try our best with you.'

Rose said, 'It's going to storm. Why don't I take you home and we can talk about this in the morning?'

'I don't care about the storm. I don't want to go home. You girls stick me there.'

I said, 'We don't stick you there, Daddy. It's the nicest house, and you live there. You've lived there all your life.'

'Let me take you home.' Rose's tone was wheedling.

I urged him. 'It's been a long day. Go with her, and then tomorrow we can –'

'No! I'd rather stay out in the storm. If you think I haven't done that before, my girl, you'd be surprised.'

A wave of exasperation washed over me. I said, 'Fine. Do what you want. You will anyway.'

'Spoken like the bitch you are!'

Rose said, 'Daddy!'

He leaned his face toward mine. 'You don't have to drive me around any more, or cook the goddammed breakfast or clean the goddammed house.' His voice modulated into a scream. 'Or tell me what I can do and what I can't do. You barren whore! I know all about you, you slut. You've been creeping here and there all your life, making up to this one and that one. But you're not really a woman, are you? I don't know what you are, just a bitch, is all, just a dried-up whore bitch.' I admit that I was transfixed; yes, I thought, this is what he's been thinking all these years, waiting to say it. For the moment, shock was like a clear window that separated us. Spittle formed in the corners of his mouth, but if it flew, I didn't feel it. Nor did I step back. Over Daddy's shoulder I saw Ty, also transfixed, unmoving, hands in pockets. Then Pete turned the corner and drove up in his own pickup.

Rose said, 'This is beyond ridiculous. Daddy, you can't mean those things. This has got to be senility talking, or Alzheimer's or something. Come on, Pete and I will take you home. You can apologize to Ginny in the morning.' Pete turned out his headlights and got out of the truck, his voice, sounding flat and distant, said, 'What's up?'

'Don't you make me out to be crazy! I know your game! The next step is the county home, with that game.'

'I'm not making you out to be crazy, Daddy. I want you to go to your house, and for things to be the way they were. You've got to stop drinking and do more work around the place. Ginny thinks so, and I think so even more than she does. I'm not going to put up with even so much as she does. We do our best for you, and have stuck with you all our lives. You can't just roll over us. You may be our father, but that doesn't give you the right to say anything you want to Ginny or to me.'

'It's you girls that make me crazy! I gave you everything, and I get nothing in return, just some orders about doing this and being that and seeing points of view.'

Rose stood like a fence post, straight, unmoved, her arms crossed over her chest. 'We didn't ask for what you gave us. We never asked for what you gave us, but maybe it was high time we got some reward for what we gave you! You say you know all about Ginny, well, Daddy, I know all about you, and you know I know. This is what we've got to offer, this same life, nothing more nothing less. If you don't want it, go elsewhere. Get someone else to take you in, because I for one have had it.' Her voice was low but penetrating, as deadly serious as ice picks.

Zadie Smith

From *White Teeth* (2000)

White Teeth interweaves the lives of three families living in the London Borough of Brent towards the end of the 20th century. Bangladeshi Samad Iqbal has a friend in Archie Jones through their shared wartime experiences. Their respective children, twins Millat and Magid Iqbal, and half-Jamaican Irie Jones, attend the same comprehensive school where they will meet, and become influenced by, the Chalfen family, outwardly the model of middle-class intellectual respectability. Smith is energetically mocking and satiric in her treatment of the complex multiracial world she depicts: in this extract Samad is collecting his young sons from an orchestral practice; despite his attempts to live as a good Muslim, he is attracted to the music teacher.

'Say "Hello, Mr Iqbal."'

'HELLO MR ICK-BALL,' came the resounding chorus from all but two of the musicians.

'Now: don't we want to play thrice as well because we have an audience?'

'YES, MISS BURT-JONES.'

And not only is Mr Iqbal our audience for today, but he's a very *special* audience. It's because of Mr Iqbal that we won't be playing *Swan Lake* any more.'

A great roar met this announcement, accompanied by a stray chorus of trumpet hoots, drum rolls, a cymbal.

'All right, all right, enough. I didn't expect *quite* so much joyous approval.'

Samad smiled. She had humour, then. There was wit there, a bit of sharpness – but why think the *more* reasons there were to sin, the *smaller* the sin was? He was thinking like a Christian again; he was saying *Can't say fairer than that* to the Creator.

'Instruments down. Yes, *you*, Marvin. *Thank you* very much.'

'What'll we be doin instead, then, Miss?'

'Well ...' began Poppy Burt-Jones, the same half-coy, half-daring smile he had noticed before. 'Something *very* exciting. Next week I want to try to experiment with some *Indian* music.'

The cymbal player, dubious of what place he would occupy in such a radical change of genre, took it upon himself to be the first to ridicule the scheme. 'What, you mean that Eeeee EEEEAAaaaa EEEeeee AAOoooo music?' he said, doing a creditable impression of the strains to be found at the beginning of a Hindi musical, or in the back-room of an 'Indian' restaurant, along with attendant head movements. The class let out a blask of laughter as loud as the brass section and echoed the gag en masse: *Eeee Eaaaoo OOOAaaah Eeee OOOiiiiiiiii*

...

'I don't think –' began Poppy Burt-Jones, trying to force her voice above the hoo-hah, then, raising it several decibels, 'I DON'T THINK IT IS VERY NICE TO –' and here her voice slipped back to normal as the class registered the angry tone and quietened down. 'I don't think it is very nice to make fun of *somebody else's culture.*'

The orchestra, unaware that this is what they had been doing, but aware that this was the most heinous crime in the Manor School rule book, looked to their collective feet.

'Do *you*? Do *you*? How would *you* like it, Sophie, if someone made fun of Queen?'

Sophie, a vaguely retarded twelve-year-old covered from head to toe in that particular rock band's paraphernalia, glared over a pair of bottle-top spectacles.

'Wouldn't like it, Miss.'

'No, you wouldn't, would you?'

'No, Miss.'

'Because Freddie Mercury is from *your culture.*'

Samad had heard the rumours that ran through the rank and file of the Palace waiters to the effect that this Mercury character was in actual fact a very light-skin Persian called Farookh, whom the head chef remembered from school in Panchgani, near Bombay. But who wished to split hairs? Not wanting to stop the lovely Burt-Jones while she was in something of a flow, Samad kept the information to himself.

'Sometimes we find other people's music strange because their culture is different from *ours*,' said Miss Burt-Jones solemnly. 'But that doesn't mean it isn't equally good, now does it?'

'NO, MISS.'

'And we can learn about each other through each other's culture, can't we?'

'YES, MISS.'

'For example, what music do you like, Millat?'

Millat thought for a moment, swung his saxophone to his side and began fingering it like a guitar. 'Bo-orn to ruuun! Da da da da daaa! Bruce Springsteen, Miss! Da da da da daaa! Baby, we were bo-orn –'

'Umm, nothing – nothing else? Something you listen to *at home,* maybe?'

Millat's face fell, troubled that his answer did not seem to be the right one. He looked over to his father, who was gesticulating wildly behind the teacher, trying to convey the jerky head and hand movements of bharata natyam, the form of dance Alsana had once enjoyed before sadness weighed her heart, and babies tied down her hands and feet.

'Thriiii-ller!' sang Millat, full throated, believing he had caught his father's gist. 'Thriii-ller night! Michael Jackson, Miss! Michael Jackson!'

Samad put his head in his hands. Miss Burt-Jones looked queerly at the small child standing on a chair, gyrating and grabbing his crotch before her. 'OK, thank you, Millat. Thank you for sharing ... that.'

Millat grinned. 'No problem, Miss.'

Colm Tóibín

From *The Heather Blazing* (1992)

This is the story of Eamon Redmond, a man who wields power and authority in his role as a High Court judge in Dublin. His summer vacation takes him back to the Irish coast where he has spent an austere and solitary childhood, acquiring his lifelong tendency to silence and repression. The narrative interweaves his recollections of the past with the unfolding events of the summer months. The following extracts recount a childhood Christmas.

On Christmas morning he awoke early, before the first thin strip of grey dawn appeared over Vinegar Hill, and went downstairs and turned on the light in the back room. The room was still warm from the fire. He found his present from Santa Claus on the table and set about unwrapping it. It was what he had wanted: a fort in separate pieces and some soldiers. There were also several bars of chocolate.

He went back upstairs, his teeth chattering with the cold, and dressed himself. By the time his father appeared he had assembled the fort on the dining-room table. He showed his father how he had pieced it together.

It was a clear day with edges of frost on the pathway down towards the Back Road. They walked to nine o'clock Mass, meeting those coming home from eight o'clock Mass and greeting them with 'Happy Christmas' and 'Many Happy Returns'. At the bottom of Pearse Road a woman asked him what he got from Santa and he told her that he got a fort and soldiers.

They walked up the aisle of the cathedral to Our Lady's side altar, but there was no room there and they had to kneel on the ground until a woman moved over and made space for them, but there still wasn't space for Eamon on the seat and he had to sit on the foot-rest.

The preparations for the consecration began to the constant sound of coughing and shuffling, soon replaced by a reverent silence once the bells rang. He watched his father out of the corner of his eye as he opened the missal at the place where the black-edged Mass card for his mother was kept. He watched his father's lips move as he prayed, the missal still open, and his mother's smiling face, familiar, he had looked at it so many times, centred in the card and below it the date of her death – 16 August 1934 – and her age, twenty-eight. He turned away as his father closed the missal, having finished whatever prayer it was he had been saying.

They went home after Mass and had breakfast. Then his father gathered all the presents they were to take to his grandmother's house: books for his grandfather and Uncle Stephen, a scarf for his Aunt Margaret and a cardigan for his grandmother. He found some wrapping paper and sellotape and set about writing cards for each of them.

'These are from you now,' his father said, 'and you're to hand them to everybody.'

…

His grandmother came in then carrying another tray with a bottle of whiskey, a jug of water, and smaller glasses.

'Go easy on this now,' she said.

'You're a great woman,' his grandfather said.

Eamon noticed that Stephen was staring into the fire, not paying attention to what was going on in the room. He didn't take any whiskey and barely spoke when he was offered more beer.

'Come on, Tom, your song,' his grandmother said.

'I'll do Boolevogue,' he said.

'Oh, that's lovely, that's lovely, now,' his grandmother said.

He started gently in a quavering tenor voice, looking down at the floor, but after the first two lines he sang with feeling.

> 'At Boolevogue as the sun was setting
> O'er the bright May meadows of Shelmalier,
> A rebel hand set the heather blazing
> And brought the neighbours from far and near.'

By the last verses he was singing with great passion, the voice no longer quivered. They all watched him, listening intently to the story of the song as though they had never heard it before. Stephen closed his eyes as the song came to an end and hunched his shoulders.

'Singing is lovely at Christmas,' his grandmother said.

William Trevor

From *The Story of Lucy Gault* (2002)

This is a haunting and evocative tale set in the Anglo-Irish 'Big House', Lahardane. It is the summer of 1921 and the parents of eight-year-old Lucy are fearful for the family's safety: local boys have been prevented once from firing the house, but they are sure to return. Lucy cannot endure the idea of leaving the beloved place; her actions, in the context of this chaotic time in Irish history, will prove devastating for them all. This extract is taken from the opening section of the novel: Everard Gault contemplates his departure from the home that has belonged to his family for generations.

On the avenue Captain Gault wondered in what circumstances he would again move through its shadows, beneath the long arch of branches that stole most of the light. On either side of him the grass, deprived, was a modest summer growth, yellow here and there with dandelions, foxgloves withering where they had thrived in the shade. He paused for a moment when he came to the gate-lodge, where life would continue when the house was abandoned. Now that an end had come, he doubted this evening that he would ever bring his family back to live at Lahardane. The prediction came from nowhere, an unwelcome repetition of what, these last few days, he had privately denied.

On the pale clay road beyond the gates he turned to the left, the berried honeysuckle scentless now, September fuchsia in the hedges. They would not for long have to rely on Heloise's legacy. Vaguely, he saw himself in a shipping office, even though he hardly knew what the work undertaken in such places involved. It didn't much matter; any decent occupation would do. Now and again they would return, a visit to see how everything was, to keep a connection going. 'It isn't for ever,' Heloise had said last night, and had spoken of the windows opened again, the dust sheets lifted, fires lit, flowerbeds weeded. And he'd said no, of course not.

In Kilauran he conversed with the deaf and dumb fisherman, as he had learnt to in his childhood: gestures made, words mouthed. They said good-bye. 'Not for too long,' he left his silent promise behind, and felt a falsehood compounded here too. He stood for a while on the rocks where sea-pinks grew in clumps. The surface of the sea was a dappled sheen, streaked with the last faint afterglow of sunset. Its waves came softly, hardly touched with foam. There was no other movement on it anywhere.

Had he been right not to reveal to Heloise, or to his child, the finality he had begun to sense in this departure? Should he have gone back to that family in Enniseala to plead a little longer? Should he have offered more than he had, whatever was felt might settle the misdemeanour he had committed, accepting that the outrage of that night was his and not the trespassers' who had come? Climbing down the rocks on to the shingle, shuffling over it to the sand, he didn't know. He didn't know when he walked on, lingering now and again to gaze out at the empty sea. He might have said to himself on this last night that he had too carelessly betrayed the past, and then betrayed, with easy comforting, a daughter and a wife. He was the one who was closest to place and people, whose love of leftover land, of house and orchard and garden, of sea and seashore, fostered instinct and premonition. Yet when he searched his feelings there was nothing there to guide him, only confusion and contradiction.

He turned towards the cliffs, crunching over the shingle again. Lost for a while in the trees, his house re-appeared, a light coming on in an upstairs window. His foot caught on something among the stones and he bent to pick it up.

Barry Unsworth

From *Morality Play* (1995)

A group of strolling players travel across a winter landscape to play their part in the Christmas revelry of a great nobleman. It is the 14th century and they inhabit a world of fear, plague and superstition. Performing their morality play of the Fall of Man, they hear of the murder of a young boy, and the ensuing accusations and rumours. They come to realise that they can use their art both to enact and resolve the crime. This is a radical notion; scriptural stories are the only subjects sanctioned for performance. Their debate becomes a complex exploration of the roles of truth and fiction. In this extract, the narrator is a runaway priest who has joined them; Martin is the chief of the players.

Martin glanced around at us once more, but briefly. His expression was calm now, and grave. 'Good people', he said, 'we must play the murder.'

These words brought a silence to the world, or so at least it seemed to me. There was no sound among us, our bodies were still. Outside in the yard the clatter of hoofs and the sound of voices were hushed also – or I became for the moment deaf to them. When silence falls on the world there is always one small sound that grows louder. I could hear the whispering and sighing of the snow and this sound was within me and without.

It was Tobias who brought the sounds back again; they came with his voice. 'Play the murder?' he said. On his face was an expression of bewilderment. 'What do you mean? Do you mean the murder of the boy? Who plays things that are done in the world?'

'It was finished when it was done,' Straw said. He paused for a moment or two, glancing round into the corners of the barn with his prominent and excitable eyes. 'It is madness,' he said. 'How can men play a thing that is only done once? Where are the words for it?' And he raised both hands and fluttered his fingers in the gesture of chaos.

'The woman who did it is still living,' Margaret said. 'If she is still living, she is in the part herself, it is hers, no one else can have it.'

I had never heard Margaret speak before in any matter concerning the playing, but Martin did not reprove her; he was too intent on the argument. 'Why should it make a difference?' he said. 'Cain killed Abel, that was a murder, it is something that happened and it only happened once. But we can play it, we play it often, we play also the manner of its doing, we put a cracked pitcher inside Abel's smock to make the smash of his bones. Why cannot we play this town's murder, since we find ourselves here?'

Tobias was shaking his head. 'There is no authority for it,' he said. 'It is not written anywhere. Cain and Abel are in the Bible.'

'Tobias is right,' I said. I could not keep silent though it meant going against Martin. What he proposed was impious and I felt fear at it. In this I sensed a difference from the others. They were astounded because the idea was new but they were not troubled in soul, except perhaps for Tobias – though this would come later to all. 'In Holy Writ there is sanction,' I said. 'The story of Cain and Abel is completed by the wisdom of God, it is not only a murder, it has its continuing in the judgement. It is encompassed within the will of the Creator.'

'So is this one, and so are all the murders of the world,' Springer said, and his thin face – face of the eternal orphan – already had the light on it of Martin's idea.

'True,' I said, 'but in this one there is no common acceptance, God has not given us this story to use, He has not revealed to us the meaning of it. So it has no meaning, it is only a death. Players are like other men, they must use God's meanings, they cannot make meanings of their own, that is heresy, it is the source of all our woes, it is the reason our first parents were cast out.'

'But already, looking round at their faces, I knew that my argument would fail. They were in some fear perhaps, but it was not fear of offending God, it was fear of the freedom Martin was holding out, the licence to play anything in the world. Such licence brings power … Yes, he offered us the world, he played; Lucifer to us there in the cramped space of the barn. But the closer prize he did not need to offer, it was already there in all our minds: the people would flock to see their murder played; and they would pay. In the end it was our destitution that won the day for him. That and the habit of mind of players, who think of their parts and how best to do them, and listen to the words of the master-player, but do not often think of the meaning as a whole. Had these done so, they would have seen what I, more accustomed to conclusions, saw and trembled at: if we make our own meanings, God will oblige us to answer our own questions, He will leave us in the void without the comfort of His Word.

4 | Critical approaches

- What is critical theory?

- Is human nature a myth?

- Is reading a political act?

Part 2 offered ways in which novels can be analysed, looking at narrative point of view, structure, types of closure and so on. As well as this type of approach, emphasising the nature of the genre, novels can also be assessed in the light of recent trends in critical thinking. Very different interpretations of a given text can result.

Different interpretations: *A Thousand Acres*

As an example, Jane Smiley's *A Thousand Acres* lends itself to *intertextual* investigation because the plot derives from Shakespeare's *King Lear*. A *narratologist* approach concentrates exclusively on the text as text – its patterns, structure, relations with other texts – rather than its content. So it would be possible to explore the connections between Smiley's novel and Shakespeare's play in terms of the echoes of the earlier text in the novel. Text and form is the emphasis here; the novel does not come bearing a 'message' for the reader. Yet, clearly a *feminist* perspective would seem equally relevant: the novelist has altered the Shakespearean source material to make the two elder sisters victims of their father's cruelty and rape. Their mother has not been able to protect them from his beatings and Smiley suggests that the social and domestic world of the American mid-west is aggressively male. The initial American reviewers of the novel often saw it as an *environmentalist* work, written with the intention of exploring the agricultural crisis of the 1980s, attacking the abuse of the land with pesticides and the factory-farming methods of rearing livestock. To these readers, the novel brought with it a warning that nature should not be violated.

Smiley's novel is not, then, the same work for all readers. American readers respond to the relationship between man and the land in the light of a long tradition, dating back to pioneer discoveries and settlements – Smiley alludes to the history of the 'thousand acres' within the novel to establish this heritage. Non-American readers who do not share this perspective will see the novel differently. It is characteristic of contemporary writing on the novel that plural readings, equally justifiable, can emerge.

▶ Read the extract from *A Thousand Acres* on pages 92–94 and reflect on your reaction to it in the light of the sexual abuse the two daughters have suffered. How does this colour your interpretation? As an alternative, read Lear's curse on Goneril in Shakespeare's play (*King Lear*, Act I, Scene 4, lines 273–287) and discuss the role of the play in Smiley's novel. (You might like to look also at the final scene in Act II of *King Lear* by way of comparison.)

Questioning the timelessness of literature

Perhaps the one area of agreement between different types of critical thinking would be that there is no single fixed and absolute interpretation of a given text. Rather, meaning and interpretation will depend on social and cultural circumstances which inevitably shift and change. Equally, critical theorists query whether there can be any fixed notions of 'human nature'. The idea that fiction transcends time and place, enshrining universal truths about the human condition, has been rejected by many contemporary schools of critical thinking. This is generally known as *anti-essentialist*. Peter Barry explains the significance of this in terms of the 'universalist' claims made for Thomas Hardy's novels:

> If we claim that great literature has a timeless and universal significance we thereby demote or disregard cultural, social, regional, and national differences in experience and outlook, preferring instead to judge all literature by a single, supposedly 'universal', standard. Thus, for instance, a routine claim about the 'Wessex' setting of Hardy's novels is that it is really a canvas on which Hardy depicts and examines fundamental, universal aspects of the human condition. Thus, Hardy's books are not thought of as primarily regional or historical or masculine or white or working-class novels – they are just novels … [and] the situations depicted can stand for all possible forms of human interaction.
>
> (*Beginning Theory*, 1995)

Just as the notion of the canon has been questioned (see page 15), so too has the idea that experience and emotion is outside historical time. The feelings of, say, Billy Prior in the trenches in Pat Barker's novels, or Roddy Doyle's Paula Spencer in 1970s Dublin, or a Jamaican airman in London, 1948, are not necessarily shared by the whole of humanity. The reader's involvement and fascination might lie in difference rather than shared experience.

▶ Do you agree with Peter Barry's argument here? Is it wrong to 'judge all literature by a single, supposedly "universal" standard'? Should literature engage readers with experiences completely outside their familiar world(s)?

History and contextuality

Some writing strongly invites a **contextual** approach where the text is located firmly in its cultural moment and is seen as a document expressive of the questions – perhaps conflicts – of a specific time. McEwan's *Saturday* articulates different types of unease within contemporary society by uniting in a single day both Britain's protest against war with Iraq and the threat of individual acts of violence. Readers recognise the fear of random violence on the streets, just as they might also connect with the opening anxiety over a possibly hijacked, burning plane approaching Heathrow. The novel thus expresses a certain contemporary situation and atmosphere: a troubled, apprehensive mood which anticipates the possibility of real crisis. It may read differently at a future time.

Where *Saturday* is an evocation of the contemporary, other novelists choose a historical setting where, again, contextual knowledge of perhaps ancient conflicts is needed to clarify readers' understanding. William Trevor alludes only fleetingly to the troubled history of British rule in Ireland, but the tragic events of *The Story of Lucy Gault*, and the emotions of those involved, have been determined by the larger movements of history. Similarly, the history of apartheid casts its shadow over Lucy's story in Coetzee's *Disgrace* where the present-day world of post-apartheid South Africa is seen to be marked and tainted by the oppressive events of the past. The critic Jago Morrison defines the post-1990 novel in terms of sweeping social change, emphasising the need to place the text within its historical moment:

> What is necessarily true of all contemporary fiction, like all literature, is that it needs to be read as a product of the cultural conditions from which it emerges. The past half century has been a period of massive, multi-dimensional cultural change. Major shifts and dislocations have occurred to older notions of racial and sexual identity. The fabric of history, collective memory and social time within which, a century ago, fiction could comfortably locate itself, has been subject to profound interrogation and transformation.
>
> (*Contemporary Fiction*, 2003)

Morrison defines the contemporary scene through the absence of cultural certainties and absolutes. Once, readers would have been united in perceiving national history and individual identity in predictable ways; this is no longer true.

▶ Think about Morrison's statement that modern fiction should be read 'as a product of [its] cultural conditions'. Read the extract from *Saturday* on pages 89–90 and discuss whether you agree that McEwan has identified a uniquely contemporary mood.

Post-colonialism

Post-colonialism is one recent critical approach which identifies new ways of interpreting contemporary writing, in particular offering a **critique** of the colonial relationship and a re-interpretation of racial histories. Post-colonial critics question assumptions of Western superiority and the coloniser's role, often celebrating cultural diversity. Zadie Smith's *White Teeth* is a particularly lively example of the sophistication of a post-colonial perspective in fiction, looking ironically at Indian, Jamaican, British and mixed-race attitudes. Cultural hybridity itself is being satirised.

Ondaatje's *The English Patient* is a subtle and questioning novel in terms of post-colonial perspectives as there is no dominant cultural voice: Almásy, the 'English Patient' is Hungarian and the trio stranded with him in the Italian villa are Canadian (Hana and Caravaggio) and Sikh (Kip). For Kip, the end of the Second World War has not been the triumph of Western values; it seems to him a mockery of his entire identity during the years of the war. All his energies have been dedicated to defusing bombs and mines, in order to lessen the devastation to civilians. When he hears about Nagasaki and Hiroshima he feels absolutely betrayed – this is not victory but the 'death of a civilisation' and the betrayal of ideals he had once identified with the British Empire:

> I grew up with traditions from my country, but later, more often, from *your* country. Your fragile white island that with customs and manners and books and prefects and reason somehow converted the rest of the world. You stood for precise behaviour. I knew if I lifted a tea-cup with the wrong finger I'd be banished. If I tied the wrong kind of knot in a tie I was out. Was it just ships that gave you power? Was it … because you had the histories and printing presses?

A post-colonial reading of *The English Patient* would emphasise the fascination of the English travellers for the Arab life of the desert; they find the exotic 'otherness' of this world irresistible. But despite their reverence for it, they desire to chart and possess it; theirs is the world of maps and knowledge, confident in The Geographical Society's history of exploration. The Englishman's rapacity is hinted at with the discovery of a solitary traveller, Fenelon-Barnes, whose tent contains maps, photographs of his family, and, alarmingly, beneath the bed covers 'a small Arab girl tied up, sleeping there'. Almásy, in his narrative, seeks oblivion in the desert, which he sees as a shifting world of fire and sand, the contours always changing. He longs to escape completely from history and nationality: 'Erase the family name! Erase nations!'

Ondaatje's own roots are complex (as a Sri Lankan he has Tamil, Sinhalese and Dutch roots, and he now lives in Canada) and the novel looks questioningly at the figure of the pre-war English explorer, and at the atrocities of European and American warfare. The text concludes with a brief epilogue where Kip, the Sikh sapper (now a doctor) is married with children, back in India and happily enjoying his evening meal with his family:

> At this table all of their hands are brown. They move with ease in their customs and habits.

Kip does not seek assimilation into European culture, nor does he wish for cultural hybridity; he has been bitterly disillusioned and chooses to reject even what he has loved.

▶ Read the extract from Andrea Levy's *Small Island* on pages 88–89. What is Gilbert's perspective as the colonised Jamaican, newly arrived in London?

Psychoanalytical readings

Post-colonialism is a way of thinking about fictional writing within society. It stems from a socio-historical approach to the text. Psychological or psychoanalytical investigation looks at the novel in a different light: examining feeling, the unconscious or unspoken, dream or illusion – all aspects of the individual psyche. Rather than fact and event, the world of imagery and symbol might be more significant. The theories of Freud inevitably underpin this type of analysis because it is Freud who first systematised the exploration of mental processes, identifying, for example, the 'Oedipus complex'. In Kate Atkinson's *Behind the Scenes at the Museum*, for example, Ruby has apparently forgotten the existence of her twin sister; she has repressed her memories because the trauma associated with Pearl's death is too extreme to endure. This notion of 'repression' comes from Freud, as does Ruby's 'transferred' anxiety: in her nightmares she is drowning or falling. She senses but cannot identify a space around her, 'an invisible cloud of sadness'. Pat Barker's *Regeneration* trilogy makes effective use of psychoanalysis through Rivers's role at Craiglockhart. The central conflict of the novels is the war itself, there is also considerable emphasis on the class struggle of the day but Barker can explore individual reaction and suffering through Rivers's analysis of nightmare and hallucination – the buried world of the subconscious.

▶ Read the account of Eamon's childhood Christmas from *The Heather Blazing* on pages 97–98. How far would it influence your understanding of the passage to consider a Freudian reading in which the absence of the mother is the crucial detail?

Differing critical approaches need not be mutually exclusive of course. In Roddy Doyle's *The Woman Who Walked into Doors* one of the crucial questions of the text must be – why does Paula Spencer remain with an abusive husband? A psychological interpretation would examine why she seems to accept his violence, why she perhaps blames herself for it. A feminist reading of the novel would emphasise the way in which a patriarchal Catholic society denies Paula any voice. The family life of her childhood has been violent, and the world she inhabits appears to conspire against female existence itself:

> Where I grew up … you were a slut or a tight bitch, one or the other, if you were a girl – and usually before you were thirteen. You didn't have to do anything to be a slut. If you were good-looking; if you grew up fast. If you had a sexy walk; if you had clean hair; if you had dirty hair. If you wore platform shoes and if you didn't.

Once Paula is married and in need of medical attention for the injuries she has received from her husband, she discovers that she is apparently invisible to the doctors and nurses who treat her, as she is to her parents and to the church – there is no acknowledgement of her suffering. The denial here comes from society not from within Paula. Here, then, a fruitful critical approach would question how Paula's world must impact upon the emotions of the abused individual.

Is reading political?

Since the 1970s there has been an industry of theoretical writing on the novel and radically different perspectives have emerged. To examine a text in the light of its historical and political context, to raise post-colonial questions, to be alert to feminist readings are all approaches which perceive textual interpretation as inherently political. The novel is imaginative writing, yet it emerges from a particular society with specific structures of power and authority where certain voices may have been marginalised or ignored.

Marxist readings derive from this political standpoint – that authors are inescapably conditioned by their own class and society (even if they might want to deny this) and their works are expressive of the inequalities and struggles within that society. Feminist readings emphasise patriarchal structures within society and explore the sexual politics of individual relationships within that wider, implicitly exploitative, context. Critical theorists approach texts from a variety of viewpoints but would tend to concur that texts do not have a single definitive meaning, and that interpretation itself is governed by circumstances of culture, class, gender and must change with time. Thus there can never be an entirely impartial or 'neutral' reading of a text; as Eagleton has argued, '[the] idea that there are "non-political" forms of criticism is simply a myth which furthers certain political uses of literature all the more effectively' (*Literary Theory: An Introduction*, 1983). For some critics, on the other hand, the reader's individual perception of the text is absolute.

Biographical or historical information about the author remains outside the text and irrelevant to it. Some academic writers have proclaimed that the high period of cultural theory is over – but that its effect cannot be ignored.

▶ As a group discussion, think about a novel you have studied and suggest different ways of interpreting it through different critical perspectives.

▶ Do you agree with Terry Eagleton that textual criticism must always be political?

5 | How to write about contemporary fiction

- How do you organise material on an entire novel?

- How do you write comparatively about two or more novels?

It's possible that you haven't previously been required to study and write on a lengthy novel; nor write comparatively about two novels. There are certain strategies which are helpful when managing a lengthy text. First, you will never be writing about every incident or conversation in a work (you would be simply reproducing the entire novel if you did). You will always be selecting *key passages* which seem to define the character of the work. When you have completed your first reading of your prescribed or chosen novel, it is worth noting these significant aspects of the work. They might be particular moments of individual revelation or insight, involving a character's understanding (or misunderstanding); or they might be a notable exchange between characters. They might well be highly charged emotionally. Think, then, about how these episodes fit into the framework of the novel as a whole.

Titles and openings

Give some thought to what the author has suggested in the *title* of the work. What kind of statement does it make? Is it a cryptic title inviting the reader's speculation? A good example would be Louis Begley's *Lies of Silence*. Whose lies does he mean? Can a lie be silent? Morally, lies are unacceptable. Is this morality irrelevant in the (Holocaust) context of the novel? What effect has it had upon the protagonist, to become a liar? Writers often choose a fragment of literary quotation as an evocative title. O'Hagan's *Be Near Me* alludes to Tennyson's *In Memoriam*, a Victorian poem which mourns the early death of a beloved friend. Does this shed light upon the central character of the text? Should the entire work be seen in the light of an elegy for lost love? O'Hagan prints part of Tennyson's poem as an *epigraph* at the beginning of the text: why?

Look closely at the *opening* of the text. How has the author drawn the reader into the novel? What questions are invited? What tone is established? What type of language is used? Who is the narrator? Is the setting past/present/future? How do you know? Go back to the opening when you are familiar with the entire text. What did you fail to notice initially? Has the writer played any tricks upon the reader? Why has the novel commenced at precisely that point? Ian McEwan's *Saturday* starts with Henry Perowne's anxieties over a burning aircraft (see pages 89–90). His fears are soon dispelled by the radio news which establishes that it has been a cargo plane with an engine fire, no one has been hurt and the plane has successfully landed at Heathrow. Why, then, does McEwan begin in this way? The plane will have no effect at all on the subsequent events of the novel. What other intention might there be?

Similarly, analyse what type of *closure* characterises your text. Does it seem open-ended? In contemporary fiction it is unlikely that the reader will encounter an ending of the 'all lived happily ever after' variety. Why not?

Genre and style

Does your text appear to conform to a specific *genre*? If it is a gothic novel, for example, would you then have certain specific expectations of a generic kind? (Science fiction, dystopia, **satire** and magic realism are other types of contemporary genres.)

How would you define the *style* of the work? The writer's choice of style might reveal a great deal about his intention. Read, for example, the extract from *The Story of Lucy Gault* (pages 98–100), where William Trevor's style is poetic and evocative. His subject is loss – a lost child and a lost way of life – so his nostalgic tone is appropriate. Style and theme combine to create the overall effect of the novel.

You should be in a position where you have analysed what constitutes the specific individuality of your chosen text: what makes it uniquely itself. As *reader*, what do you find engaging – or perhaps repellent – about this work? If you are, indeed, troubled or revolted by the writing, can you define why? Bear in mind that contemporary writing is controversial: the subject matter of Ishiguro's *Never Let Me Go* has been seen as disturbing by many readers but it is widely perceived as an important work. Clearly, books are written and read for reasons beyond offering pleasurable entertainment. Ishiguro's novel prompts readers to speculate why it has been written.

Structuring the essay

If you are defining for yourself the area of your written assignment, then use your choice to select what has most interested you in the writing. *Structure* your essay by thinking about which selected passages best convey the subject you are debating. Think carefully about the order in which you wish to discuss these: chronologically might seem to make most sense, but could veer dangerously close to summarising the text. Don't mistake description for analysis. Begin with an iconic moment – one which seems representative of the entire mood

Reviews of Ishiguro's novel tended to concur in regarding it as a major, important work. *Time* lists it in its 'All-Time 100 novels of the 20th century'. Initial reviewers of Zadie Smith's *White Teeth*, on the other hand, were often divided in their assessment. Read the following extracts, bearing in mind your own impressions of the novel.

> *White Teeth* is so unlike the kind of comic novel currently in vogue among young British women – the girl-about-town Bridget Jones wannabe – that its very willingness to look beyond the stock in trade of boyfriends and weight problems is a mark of distinction. Smith's real talent emerges not just in her voice but in her ear, which enables her to inhabit characters of different generations, races and mind-sets. Whether it's her notation of Archie's blokish colloquialisms ('Blimey!', 'I should cocoa'), Clara's Anglo-Jamaican patois ('Sno prob-lem. If you wan' help: jus' arks farrit'), the banter of two ancient Jamaican grouches or of second-generation Bengali teenagers, the mongrel texture of metropolitan life rises vividly from the page. There is more than virtuosity at work here. Smith likes her characters, and while she is alert to their shortcomings and blind spots, her generosity toward them never flags.
>
> That is why *White Teeth*, for all its tensions, is a peculiarly sunny novel. Its crowdedness, its tangle of competing voices and viewpoints, betoken a society, and a time in which miscegenation is no longer the exception but the norm: 'It is only this late in the day that you can walk into a playground and find Isaac Leung by the fish pond, Danny Rahman in the football cage, Quang O'Rourke bouncing a basketball and Irie Jones humming a tune. Children with first and last names on a direct collision course.' There are reasons, so late in the day, to be cheerful, and this eloquent, wit-struck book is not least among them.
>
> (Anthony Quinn in the *New York Times*, 30 April 2000)

> Bad writers, young or old, never seem to understand that any information imparted – be it descriptive or conversational – should be justifiable, not merely an exercise in preening. In short, Smith is incapable of writing about something in fifteen to twenty words if a hundred can do – this is the unmistakable hallmark of a bad writer.
>
> ... *White Teeth* reads sort of like one of those randy British films that went abysmally wrong – think *The Full Monty* gone Southern Gothic grotesque. Too many scenes read like wan sketches or ideas that are on a to do list that is never picked up on again, and there are far too many actual lists within the book, such as a list of Millat's and Alsana's possessions, which serves no purpose in the tale, save to show 'cultural awareness'. Many other scenes stand nakedly

embarrassing in their content and detail, as Smith cannot even string a single full narrative paragraph together. It's as if she had ADD [Attention Deficit Disorder], or was a filmmaker with a shaky hand held camera. In the end, this disjointed, unreadable mess is merely a wannabe underground Baedeker to London, yet it has no index page, for Smith was too lazy to include even that gratuity. *White Teeth* is a bad, bad, novel, with little redeeming about it, and Smith will have a long way to go if she is even going to approach middle brow mediocrity as a writer.

(Dan Schneider in *Hackwriters, the International Writers' Magazine*, April 2007)

▶ Is there any reason why *White Teeth* should invite the vitriolic attack of the second review? What is your own opinion?

▶ Zadie Smith's style invites very different responses here. Reread the extract on pages 95–97 and define what you find compelling, or unsuccessful, about Smith's narrative voice.

▶ Anthony Quinn, in common with many reviewers, has found the cultural hybridity of *White Teeth* both comic and celebratory. What is your own view?

▶ Suggest whether other post-1990 novels you have studied might produce reviews so radically at odds with each other. In group discussion, you might propose, and defend, different opinions.

Assignments

The following assignments are intended to provoke thought on different types of contemporary fiction. They may suggest subjects for written assignments or for discussion. Most can be adapted to your own choice of reading.

1 'Fictions, if successful, make sense of the here and now' (Frank Kermode in *The Sense of an Ending*). Select a novel you feel to be particularly expressive of the contemporary world and discuss how it engages with modern life.

2 When Coetzee was voted winner of the *Observer's* best work of contemporary British fiction (October 2006), Robert McCrum, literary editor of the *Observer*, wrote 'As readers, we want our "great novels" to include as much as possible of experience and to address the great issues of our time.' Think about how a novel such as Coetzee's *Disgrace* or Ishiguro's *Never Let Me Go* addresses serious contemporary issues.

3 'The Somme is like the Holocaust. It revealed things about mankind that we *cannot* come to terms with and cannot forget. It never becomes the past' (Pat Barker). Examine Barker's or other writers' novels about the First World War in the light of this statement.

4 Starting with the extract from Barry Unsworth's *Morality Play* (pages 100–101), think about ways in which novels can evoke a distant and unfamiliar past.

5 Study the use of a child narrator in one or more novels and consider the ways in which the author has conveyed a child's perspective.

6 Post-1990 fiction has been described as 'a fruitful space in which the politics of identity could be explored' (Nick Bentley *British Fiction of the 1990s*). Think about a novel such as Zadie Smith's *White Teeth* or Andrea Levy's *Small Island* and examine the text's engagement with 'politics of identity'.

7 Linden Peach writes about the role of the novel in exploring taboo
   subjects such as marital violence or child abuse: ' … subjects that have
   been marginalised … topics that have been silenced' (*The Contemporary
   Irish Novel*). Analyse how any one text (or author) has chosen to approach
   this type of subject matter.

8 Malcolm Bradbury has found in post-1990 fiction 'an anxious atmosphere
   of disorder, terror or gothic extremity'. Think about any of the novels
   written as a response to the 9/11 attacks on New York (Jay McInerney,
   de Lillo, Cormac McCarthy) and discuss the fictional presentation of
   apocalyptic anxiety.

9 The Czech novelist Milan Kundera writes of the novel's ability to 'unmask
   the secret life of the feelings'. Study closely any novel which seems to
   you to explore this 'secret life' and discuss how the author has chosen to
   disclose the inner world.

10 The contemporary novel is often seen as strikingly experimental in form
    and language. Consider any text you judge to be artistically challenging;
    analyse its fictional methods and suggest why the author has chosen to
    write in an unconventional way.

11 Get together with a group of students studying post-1990 fiction and
    propose your own 'Booker shortlist' of contemporary novels, giving
    reasons for your choice of titles.

12 Research a range of reviews of one or more novels. Discuss whether or
    not you agree with the opinions expressed by the reviewers. Write your
    own review of a recent novel.

6 | Resources

Further reading

There are a number of excellent studies of the novel, sections of which are relevant to post-1990 writing. Jane Smiley's *Thirteen Ways of Looking at the Novel* (Faber & Faber, 2006) is full of insights into both writing and reading contemporary fiction. David Lodge *The Art of Fiction* (Penguin Books, 1992) offers brief discussion of a number of narrative techniques, as does John Mullan's *How Novels Work* (Oxford University Press, 2006). Mullan's textual examples are all drawn from post-1990 novels. Jeremy Hawthorn's *Studying the Novel* (5th edition, 2005, Oxford University Press) is a scholarly work intended for undergraduate study; it is an excellent account of theory and genre, textual illustration here being drawn from a range of fictional writing rather than concentrating on the contemporary.

A first-class introduction to critical theory would be Peter Barry's *Beginning Theory* (Manchester University Press, 1995). Two dependable dictionaries of literary terms are: M.H. Abrams *A Glossary of Literary Terms* (Holt, Rinehart and Winston, 5th edition, 1988) and J.A. Cuddon *The Penguin Dictionary of Literary Terms and Literary Theory* (Penguin Books, 1998).

A number of studies of contemporary British fiction have appeared in recent years. These tend to be organised in terms of an introduction to the field followed by chapters on individual writers or specific themes. You may find helpful chapters in any of the following:

James Acheson and Sarah Ross *The Contemporary British Novel* (Edinburgh University Press, 2005)

Nick Bentley (ed.) *British Fiction of the 1990s* (Routledge, 2005)

John Brannigan *Orwell to the Present: Literature in England, 1945–2000* (Palgrave, 2003)

Peter Childs *Contemporary Novelists* (Palgrave, 2005)

Richard Lane, Rod Mengham, Philip Tew *Contemporary British Fiction* (Polity Press, 2003)

Rod Mengham (ed.) *An Introduction to Contemporary Fiction* (Polity Press, 1999)

Linden Peach *The Contemporary Irish Novel* (Palgrave, 2004)

Brian Shaffer *Reading the Novel in English 1950–2000* (Blackwell, 2006)

Philip Tew *The Contemporary British Novel* (Continuum, 2004)

Websites

The Internet is a useful tool when researching contemporary writing. Use official sites which will be dependably accurate. Reviews and online interviews often provide a valuable starting point for discussion and these can often be found through the principal arts' pages of the press, e.g. http://books.guardian.co.uk. If you have access to a good academic library then Literature Online is a superb resource. The British Council website also offers helpful discussions of contemporary writers: www.contemporarywriters.com. Follow the link for your chosen author.

Individual authors tend to have excellent official sites, e.g. www.ianmcewan.com

Information about recent political or cultural events can be readily found on the BBC website.

Glossary of critical terms

Closure the ending to a work of fiction, usually denoting a degree of finality. Contemporary writing is more likely to exploit reader expectation and conclude in an open-ended way.

Codex originally a volume of manuscript, now a book with pages.

Contextuality the social, historical, cultural context of a work.

Critique a work of literature may be said to offer a critique of its society (or some aspect of it) where it is assessing and questioning established structures and attitudes.

Epigraph a quotation which precedes a literary work, usually printed after the author's dedication and any acknowledgements. It might be a fragment from a poem or song and it has some imaginative connection with the work.

Frame narrator see **Narrator**

Genre literally, type: literature can be broadly identified as poetry, drama or fiction. There are also sub-genres such as biography, travel writing, science fiction, etc.

Gothic novel a genre first associated with novels of mystery and the supernatural at the end of the eighteenth century. Contemporary writing, such as Patrick McCabe's, is said to be gothic because it incorporates challenging depictions of violence and horror.

Intertextuality in critical theory, the idea that all texts connect with previous texts; some writers experiment with this idea by weaving pre-existing texts into their novels – Michael Cunningham's *The Hours* is a good example.

Magic realism combining an effect of fantasy or the bizarre with everyday realism: the opening of Rushdie's *Satanic Verses* is a classic example.

Metafiction fiction which is about fiction: the author chooses to remind readers that they are engaged with the artifice of literature. At the end of David Lodge's novel *Changing Places* the author comments on the fact that the reader must be aware of the impending end because of the 'tell-tale compression of the pages'.

Narrative in general terms the recounting of any sequence of events, real or fictional. In terms of the novel, the story itself.

Narrator the teller of the tale, whether first-person narrator or third-person, omnisicient narrator. **Frame narrator** describes the initial narrator who may then disappear for the chief part of the text, to return at the end of the tale. Modern writing often makes use of the device of an unreliable narrator where the reader sees beyond what is recounted by the principal narrator. The narrator is not to be confused with the author.

Paratext the term used for any material outside the narrative, but connected to it: title, epigraph, dedication, publisher's blurb, comments from critics or reviewers. This material colours the readers' approach to the narrative itself.

Pastiche an imitation of a literary style or author.

Postmodernism postmodernist writing is characteristically experimental and anti-realist, often questioning whether 'reality' can be said to exist in a world dominated by huge anonymous forces of commerce and technology.

Protagonist principal character of the fiction.

Satire literature which intends to mock the follies or vices of society, often through exaggeration and ridicule.

Verisimilitude literally, true to life and usually associated with realist fiction where the author wants to convey an impression of life as it is lived.

Chronology of events and books discussed

	Historical/cultural events	Titles cited in this text
1990	'Poll Tax' riots in London; resignation of Thatcher (succeeded as PM by John Major); East and West Germany reunified	A.S. Byatt *Possession;* Hanif Kureishi *The Buddha of Suburbia;* Brian Moore *Lies of Silence*
1991	First war against Iraq in the Gulf; Britain opts out of European single currency; break up of the Soviet Union	Angela Carter *Wise Children*; Jane Smiley *A Thousand Acres*; Pat Barker *Regeneration*; Louis Begley *Wartime Lies*
1992	Conservatives win general election; Polytechnics given university status; creation of the World Wide Web	Michael Ondaatje *The English Patient*; Colm Tóibín *The Heather Blazing*; Patrick McCabe *The Butcher Boy*
1993	IRA bomb in Warrington; first IRA cease-fire; killing of James Bulger	Irvine Welsh *Trainspotting*; Sebastian Faulks *Birdsong*; Annie Proulx *The Shipping News*
1994	Church of England first ordains women priests; Nelson Mandela first black President of South Africa: end of apartheid	James Kelman *How Late It Was, How Late*; Hilary Mantel *A Change of Climate*; Jonathan Coe *What a Carve Up!*
1995	Channel Tunnel opened; NATO bombing campaign against Serb artillery followed by ceasefire in Bosnia; head teacher Philip Lawrence murdered outside his school in west London	Barry Unsworth *Morality Play*; Pat Barker *The Ghost Road*; Kate Atkinson *Behind the Scenes at the Museum*; Patrick McCabe *The Dead School*; Penelope Fitzgerald *The Blue Flower*
1996	IRA bomb at Canary Wharf; divorce of Prince and Princess of Wales; opening of Shakespeare's Globe Theatre by the Thames	Roddy Doyle *The Woman Who Walked into Doors*

1997	Election victory for 'New Labour'; Tony Blair Prime Minister; death of Diana, Princess of Wales, in car crash in Paris; Hong Kong returned to China	Ian McEwan *Enduring Love*; Jim Crace *Quarantine*
1998	Northern Ireland Good Friday agreement between Ulster Unionists and Sinn Fein; Andrew Motion succeeds Ted Hughes as Poet Laureate	Ian McEwan *Amsterdam*; Julian Barnes *England, England*; Pat Barker *Another World*; Michael Cunningham *The Hours*
1999	Scottish Parliament and Welsh Assembly open; 'ethnic cleansing' in former Yugoslavia; UK does not adopt Euro currency	J.M. Coetzee *Disgrace*; Colm Tóibín *The Blackwater Lightship*
2000	Millennium celebrations at the 'Dome' in Greenwich; inauguration of George Bush Jnr as Republican President of the USA	Zadie Smith *White Teeth*
2001	Terrorists destroy World Trade Center in New York; Labour re-elected with Blair as PM	Ian McEwan *Atonement*; Jonathan Coe *The Rotters' Club*
2002	Golden Jubilee of Elizabeth II; US invasion of Afghanistan	William Trevor *The Story of Lucy Gault*; Michael Frayn *Spies*; Yann Martel *The Life of Pi*; Robert Edric *Peacetime*
2003	Invasion of Iraq by US-led coalition, backed by Tony Blair and British Government despite questions over alleged existence of Iraqi 'Weapons of Mass Destruction'	Graham Swift *The Light of Day*; Monica Ali *Brick Lane*; J.G. Ballard *Millennium People*; Mark Haddon *The Curious Incident of the Dog in the Night-Time;* Khaled Hosseini *The Kite Runner*

2004	Expansion of EU into Eastern Europe; terrorist explosions on rush-hour trains in Madrid; earthquake in SE Asia causes tsunami waves and numbers of deaths	Andrea Levy *Small Island*; Allan Hollinghurst *The Line of Beauty*; Jonathan Coe *The Closed Circle*
2005	Terrorist bombings in London; Kyoto protocol on climate change; death of Pope John Paul II	Kazuo Ishiguro *Never Let Me Go*; Ian McEwan *Saturday*; Julian Barnes *Arthur and George*; Zadie Smith *On Beauty*
2006	Saddam Hussein found guilty of crimes against humanity and sentenced to death (hanged December 2006); Tony Blair announces that he will step down as Labour leader; alleged terrorist plot involving aircraft travelling between UK and USA	Anne Tyler *Digging to America*; Cormac McCarthy *The Road*; Jay McInerney *The Good Life*; Sarah Waters *The Night Watch*; Andrew O'Hagan *Be Near Me;* David Mitchell *Black Swan Green*, Kiran Desai *The Inheritance of Loss*; Roddy Doyle *Paula Spencer*
2007	Blair succeeded by Gordon Brown as Leader of the Labour Party and PM; Salman Rushdie awarded a Knighthood; celebrations of 60 years of Indian Independence	Robert Edric *The Kingdom of Ashes*; Don DeLillo *Falling Man*

Index

Sage, Lorna 18, 82–3
Sassoon, Siegfried 32, 54
satire 22, 110, 121
Schneider, Dan 116
Sebald, W.G. 30
secrets 72–4
Shaffer, Brian 19
Shakespeare, William: comedies 57–8,
    84–5; *King Lear* 38, 48–9, 92–4, 102;
    Tempest 38
Smiley, Jane: *Thirteen Ways* 13–14, 35–6,
    50, 119; *Thousand Acres* 7, 38, 48–9,
    92–4, 102–3
Smith, Zadie 6–7, 19; *On Beauty* 38–9;
    London 7, 18, 20, 23, 61, 95–7; *White
    Teeth* 23, 60–1, 68–9, 74, 95–7, 105,
    115–16
Sontag, Susan 14
South Africa 18, 65–6, 85–6
Steiner, George 31
structure 70–1, 72–5, 111
style 9, 27–8, 110
Sutherland, John 11, 13
swearing 16
Swift, Graham 6, 10, 23, 51

taboo 25–8, 62
Tarantino, Quentin 25
Tew, Philip 19
Thatcherism 16, 22
Thorpe, Adam 30, 54
timelessness 103
titles 78, 109
Todd, Richard 18, 24
Tóibín, Colm 7, 17; *Blackwater Lightship*
    37; *Heather Blazing* 49–50, 63–4,
    97–8; *Master* 28
Trevor, William 7, 61; *Lucy Gault* 62–3,
    98–100, 104, 110
Tyler, Anne 21

Unsworth, Barry 29, 30, 54, 72, 100–1

verisimilitude 54, 121

war novels 27, 30–3, 55–6, 78–9, 105
Warner, Marina 38
Waters, Sarah 30, 56
website sources 120
Welsh, Irvine 6; *Trainspotting* 16, 24, 27,
    37, 38, 60
Woolf, Virginia 38, 47, 70

Acknowledgements

The authors and publishers acknowledge the following sources of copyright material and are grateful for the permissions granted. While every effort has been made, it has not always been possible to identify the sources of all the material used, or to trace all copyright holders. If any omissions are brought to our notice, we will be happy to include the appropriate acknowledgements on reprinting.

pp. 55, 91–2: Bloomsbury Publishers and Trident Media Group on behalf of the author for extracts from Michael Ondaatje, *The English Patient*, pp. 150, 255–7. Copyright © 1992 by Michael Ondaatje; pp. 113–14: Mic Cheetham Literary Agency on behalf of the author for a review of *Never Let Me Go* by M. John Harrison, *Guardian Unlimited*, 26.2.05; pp. 46–7, 87–8: Faber and Faber Ltd and Alfred A. Knopf, a division of Random House, Inc, for extracts from Kazuo Ishiguro *Never Let Me Go*, pp. 65–7, 73, 217. Copyright © 2005 by Kazuo Ishiguro; p. 83: Granta for extracts from an editorial by Ian Jacks *Granta* (56) p. 7; pp. 93–4: HarperCollins Publishers and Abner Stein on behalf of the author for an extract from Jane Smiley *A Thousand Acres*, pp. 180–2. Copyright ©1992 by Jane Smiley; pp. 49, 65–6, 85–6: David Higham Associates on behalf of the author for extracts from J. M. Coetzee *Disgrace*, Secker & Warburg (1999) pp. 1, 44, 158, 199, 205, 216–18, 218–19; pp. 113: News International Syndication for a review of *Never Let Me Go* by Peter Kemp, *Times Online*, 20.2.05. Copyright © 2005 Times Newspapers Ltd; pp. 49–50, 64, 97–8: Pan Macmillan, London, and Viking Penguin, a division of Penguin Group (USA) Inc, for extracts from Colm Tóibín *The Heather Blazing*, pp. 66–7, 72–3, 154, 170. Copyright © 1992 by Colm Tóibín; pp. 99–100, 100–1, 95–7: Penguin Books with Viking Penguin, a division of Penguin Group (USA) Inc, and SSL/Sterling Lord Literistic, Inc on behalf of the author for extracts from William Trevor *The Story of Lucy Gault*, (Penguin Books, 2002) pp. 26–8. Copyright © 2002 by William Trevor; with Doubleday, a division of Random House, Inc for extracts from Barry Unsworth *Morality Play*, (Penguin Books, 1996) pp. 63–5. Copyright © 1995, 1996 Barry Unsworth; and an extract from Zadie Smith *White Teeth* (Hamish Hamilton, 2000) pp. 133–4. Copyright © 2000 by Zadie Smith; pp. 61, 69, 70, 52, 89–90: Random House Group Ltd, with Scribner, an imprint of Simon & Schuster Adult Publishing Group, for extracts from Monica Ali *Brick Lane*, Doubleday, 86–7, 215, 251, 477–578, 492; and with Nan A Talese, an imprint of The Doubleday Broadway Publishing Group, a division of Random House, Inc, for extracts from Ian McEwan *Saturday*, Jonathan Cape, pp. 14–16, 32–3. Copyright © 2005 by Ian McEwan; pp. 57, 84–5: Rogers, Coleridge & White Ltd on behalf of the author for extracts from Angela Carter *Wise Children*, Random House (1992) pp. 90, 93, 206. Copyright © 1992 Angela Carter; pp. 115–16: www.hackwriters.com and Dan Schneider, webmaster of Cosmoetica.com, for his review of *White Teeth*, Hackwriters, April, 2007